Defence and National Security of India

Concerns and Strategies

Edited by

C. Vinodan

Co-ordinator, Rajiv Gandhi Chair for Public Policy Studies
and
Honorary Director,
Institute for Contemporary Chinese Studies (ICCS),
School of International Relations and Politics,
Mahatma Gandhi University, Kottayam, Kerala

New Century Publications
New Delhi, India

NEW CENTURY PUBLICATIONS
4800/24, Bharat Ram Road,
Ansari Road, Daryaganj,
New Delhi - 110 002 (India)

Tel.: 011-2324 7798, 4358 7398, 6539 6605
Fax: 011-4101 7798
E-mail: indiatax@vsnl.com • info@newcenturypublications.com
www.newcenturypublications.com

Editorial office:
LG–7, Aakarshan Bhawan,
4754-57/23, Ansari Road, Daryaganj,
New Delhi – 110 002

Tel.: 011-4356 0919

First Published: **2017**

ISBN: **978-81-7708-440-5**

Published by New Century Publications and printed at Salasar Imaging Systems, New Delhi.

Designs: Patch Creative Unit, New Delhi.

PRINTED IN INDIA

About the Book

With a strength of over 1.3 million active personnel, India is world's third largest military force. India was the largest importer of defence equipment in 2014 with Russia, Israel, France and the United States being the top foreign suppliers of military equipment. The Government of India has launched 'Make-in-India' initiative to indigenize manufacturing and reduce dependence on imports, including defence imports and procurement.

The beginning of the 21st century saw reorientation of India on the global stage from a regional role in the sub-continent to a major role in the Indian Ocean region stretching from Gulf of Aden to the Malacca Strait. Contemporary criticisms of the Indian military have drawn attention to several issues, such as obsolete equipment, lack of adequate ammunition, and inadequate research and development due to over-reliance on foreign imports.

In the context of defence preparedness, national security means that a government should protect the state and its citizens against all kind of *national* crises through a variety of power projections such as political power, diplomacy, economic power, military might, and so on. Elements of national security include: (a) military security, (b) political security, (c) economic security, (d) environmental security, (e) security of energy and natural resources, and (f) cyber security.

National Security Council (NSC) of India is an executive government agency tasked with advising the Prime Minister's office on matters of national security and strategic interest. The three-tiered structure of the NSC comprises of the Strategic Policy Group, the National Security Advisory Board and a Secretariat represented by the Joint Intelligence Committee (JIC).

This volume contains 10 research articles, authored by experts in the field, which provide deep insights into the defence and national security preparedness and concerns of India.

About the Editor

Dr. C. Vinodan is currently Co-ordinator, Rajiv Gandhi Chair for Public Policy Studies and Honorary Director, Institute for Contemporary Chinese Studies (ICCS), School of International Relations and Politics, Mahatma Gandhi University, Kottayam, Kerala. He has worked previously at the Post-graduate and Research Department of Political Science, Sree Narayana College, Kollam and Department of Political Science, University of Kerala.

He obtained his M.A. (II Rank), M.Phil. and Ph.D. degrees in Political Science from the University of Kerala. He was awarded the Visiting Scholar Fellowship (2003) by the Claremont Graduate University, California, USA. He has attended numerous courses in international relations in India and abroad. These include the 2016 Sino-Indian Cross-Cultural Dialogues held by the Institute of Advanced International Studies, Sun Yat-sen University, Guangzhou, China; and the US Department of States Fulbright American Studies Institute (FASI) course on foreign policy at the University of Delaware, Philadelphia in 2000.

Dr. Vinodan has also attended and presented papers at various national and international conferences/seminars. He is also the recipient of a number of awards including Kerala University Post-Doctoral Award (2003-2005). He is also a member of the editorial board of the *Journal of Human Security*, *Indian Journal of Politics and International Relations* and *South Asian Journal of Diplomacy*. He has published 40 research papers and 4 books.

His areas of teaching and research activities include international relations, security studies, Chinese studies, South Asian studies, energy, environment and human security.

Contents

About the Book .... *v*
About the Editor .... *vi*
Contributors .... *ix-x*
Introduction by the Editor .... *xi-xviii*

1. India's Quest for Global Power Status in the 21st Century **1-16**
Nalini Kant Jha

2. Redefining India's Maritime Future **17-31**
P.V. Rao

3. Indian Foreign Policy 'Modi'fied: From Non-alignment to Multi-vectored Alignment **32-51**
Mohanan Bhaskaran Pillai

4. Maritime Security and Contemporary India **52-71**
S. Utham Kumar Jamadhagni

5. Maritime Threats from South of India **72-85**
Jacob Ashik Bonofer

6. India's Coastal Security: A Perspective **86-100**
Suresh R.

7. Challenges to Indian Defence Co-operation with Russia **101-117**
Zeeshan Munir

8. China Factor in India's Neighbourhood Policy **118-141**
Srikanth Thaliyakkattil

9. India and Tibetan Autonomy: A National Security Perspective **142-159**
Rakhee Viswambharan

10. India's Maritime Challenges in the South China Sea **160-188**
C. Vinodan

Index **189-196**

Contributors

Nalini Kant Jha	Dean, School of Social Sciences and International Studies and Director, Southern Asia Studies Programme, Pondicherry University, Puducherry.
P.V. Rao	Emeritus Professor of Political Science, UGC; Formerly Director, Centre for Indian Ocean Studies, Osmania University, Hyderabad.
Mohanan Bhaskaran Pillai	Professor, Department of Politics and International Studies, Pondicherry University, Puducherry.
S. Utham Kumar Jamadhagni	Associate Professor, Department of Defence and Strategic Studies, University of Madras, Chennai.
Jacob Ashik Bonofer	Assistant Professor, Department of Political Science, Madras Christian College, Chennai.
Suresh R.	Associate Professor, Department of Political Science, University of Kerala, Thiruvananthapuram.
Zeeshan Munir	Research Scholar, School of International Studies, Jawaharlal Nehru University (JNU), New Delhi.
Srikanth Thaliyakkattil	Formerly with the Department of International Relations, Peking University, Beijing.
Rakhee Viswambharan	Assistant Professor and Head, Department of Political Science, Sree Narayana College, Chempazhanthy, Thiruvananthapuram.

C. Vinodan Co-ordinator, Rajiv Gnadhi Chair for Public Policy Studies, School of International Relations and Politics, Mahatma Gandhi University, Kottyam.

Introduction by the Editor

India's Defence Forces

With a strength of over 1.3 million active personnel, India is world's 3rd largest military force and has the world's largest volunteer army. Defence forces of India consist of three professional uniformed services: Indian Army, Indian Navy, and Indian Air Force. Additionally, the Indian armed forces are supported by the three paramilitary organisations: Assam Rifles, Indian Coast Guard and Special Frontier Force. They are also supported by various inter-service commands and institutions such as the Strategic Forces Command, Andaman and Nicobar Command and Integrated Defence Staff.

The President of India is the Supreme Commander of the Indian armed forces. The armed forces are under the management of the Ministry of Defence, Government of India.

It is important to note that the Central Armed Police Forces are headed by officers from the Indian Police Service and are under the control of the Ministry of Home Affairs, not the Ministry of Defence.

The Indian armed forces have been engaged in a number of major military operations, including the Indo-Pakistan wars of 1947-48, 1965 and1971, and the Chinese aggression in 1962. Indian victory over Pakistan in the 1971 war, helped create the free country of Bangladesh.

India honours its armed forces and military personnel annually on Armed Forces Flag Day, December 7. Since 1962, the IAF has maintained close military relations with Russia, including cooperative development on programmes such as the Fifth Generation Fighter Aircraft (FGFA) and the Multirole Transport Aircraft (MTA). The Indian armed forces are steadily undergoing modernisation, with investments in areas such as missile defence system and a nuclear triad.

The Department of Defence Production of the Ministry of Defence is responsible for the indigenous production of equipment used by the Indian Armed Forces. It comprises the 41 Indian

Ordnance Factories under control of the Ordnance Factories Board.

India was the largest importer of defence equipment in 2014 with Russia, Israel, France and the United States being the top foreign suppliers of military equipment. The Government of India has launched 'Make-in-India' initiative to indigenize manufacturing and reduce dependence on imports, including defence imports and procurement.

The beginning of the 21st century saw reorientation for India in the global stage from a regional role in the subcontinent to a major role in the Indian Ocean region, stretching from Gulf of Aden to the Malacca Strait. India's sphere of influence needs to encompass not just the South Asian subcontinent, but also the northern Indian Ocean area, from the eastern seaboard of Africa in the west, to the Malacca Straits in the east, and must include Iran, Afghanistan, the Central Asian Republics (CARs), China and Myanmar. India's credibility, as a regional power will be contingent upon institutional stability, economic development and military strength, including nuclear deterrence. The long stretches of disputed borders with China and Pakistan and sizeable areas under their occupation continue to be major irritants, notwithstanding the peace processes underway with both the countries.

Indian armed forces have four main tasks:

1. To assert the territorial integrity of India.
2. To defend the country if attacked by a foreign nation.
3. To support the civil community in case of disasters (e.g., flooding).
4. To participate in United Nations peacekeeping operations in consonance with India's commitment to the United Nations Charter.

The major deployments of the Indian Army constitute the border regions of India, particularly Jammu and Kashmir, Ladakh, and the North-East India, in order to engage in counter-insurgency and anti-terrorist operations. The major commitments of the Indian Navy constitute patrol missions, anti-piracy operations off the coast of Somalia, maintaining a military presence in Southeast Asia's waters, and joint exercises with other countries.

Contemporary criticisms of the Indian military have drawn attention to several issues, such as obsolete equipment, lack of adequate ammunition, and inadequate research and development due to over reliance on foreign imports. In addition, the lack of a *strategic culture* among the political class in India is claimed to have hindered the effectiveness of the Indian military. These issues are believed by critics to hobble the progress and modernisation of the military.

Indian Air Force is the air arm of the Indian armed forces. Its primary responsibility is to secure Indian airspace and to conduct aerial surveys during a conflict. It was officially established on October 8, 1932 as an auxiliary air force of the British Raj and the prefix *Royal* was added in 1945 in recognition of its services during World War II. After India achieved Independence from the United Kingdom in 1947, the Royal Indian Air Force served the Dominion of India, with the prefix being dropped when India became a republic in 1950. The Indian Air Force plays a crucial role in securing Indian airspace and also in India's power projection in South Asia and the Indian Ocean. Therefore, modernising and expanding Indian Air Force is a top priority for the Indian government.

In recent years, the Indian Navy has undergone modernization and expansion with the intention of countering growing Chinese maritime power in the Indian Ocean and reaching the status of a recognised blue-water navy.

National Security

There is no single universally accepted definition of national security. The variety of definitions provides an overview of the many usages of this concept. The concept still remains ambiguous, having originated from simpler definitions which initially emphasised the freedom from military threat and political coercion to later increase in sophistication and include other forms of non-military security which suited the circumstances of the time.

Broadly speaking, national security means that a government, along with its parliaments, should protect the state and its citizens against all kind of *national* crises through a variety of power projections such as political power, diplomacy, economic power, military might, and so on.

The concept developed mostly in the United States after the Second World War. Initially focusing on military might, it now encompasses a broad range of facets, all of which impinge on the non-military or economic security of the nation and the values espoused by the national society. Accordingly, in order to possess national security, a nation needs to possess economic security, energy security, environmental security etc. Security threats involve not only conventional foes such as other nation-states but also non-state actors such as violent non-state actors, narcotic cartels, multinational corporations and non-governmental organisations. Some authorities include natural disasters and events causing severe environmental damage in this category.

Elements of National Security: These include the following.

A. Military Security: This is traditionally, the earliest recognised form of national security. Military security implies the capability of a nation to defend itself, and/or deter military aggression. Alternatively, military security implies the capability of a nation to enforce its policy choices by use of military force. The term *military security* is considered synonymous with *security* in much of its usage.

B. Political Security: Political security is about the stability of the social order. System referent objects are defined, such as nation-states, nations, transnational groups of political importance including tribes, minorities, some religious organisations, systems of states such as the European Union and the United Nations, besides others. Diplomacy, negotiation and other interactions form the means of interaction between the objects.

C. Economic Security: Historically, conquest of nations has made conquerors rich through plunder, access to new resources and enlarged trade by controlling the conquered nations' economy. In today's complex system of international trade, characterised by multi-national agreements, mutual inter-dependence and availability of natural resources etc., the freedom to exercise choice of policies to develop a nation's economy in the manner desired, invites economic security. Economic security today forms, arguably, as important a part of national security as military security. The creation and protection of jobs that supply defence and non-defence needs are vital to national security. Third world countries are less secured due to lack of employment for their citizens.

D. Environmental Security: Environmental security deals with environmental issues which threaten the national security of a nation in any manner. The scope and nature of environmental threats to national security and strategies to engage them is a subject of debate. While all environmental events are not considered significant of being categorised as threats, many transnational issues, both global and regional, would affect national security. These can be classified as under:

- **Transnational Environmental Problems:** These include global environmental problems such as climate change due to global warming, deforestation and loss of biodiversity etc.
- **Environmental Problems that Threaten a Nation's Security:** These would be problems whose outcomes would result in conventional threats to national security as first or higher order outcomes. Such disputes could range from heightened tension or outright conflict due to disputes over water scarcity in the Middle East, to illegal immigration into the United States caused by the failure of agriculture in Mexico. The genocide in Rwanda, indirectly or partly caused by rise in population and dwindling availability of farmland, is an example of the extremity of outcome arising from problems of environmental security.
- **Environmentally Threatening Outcomes of Warfare:** For example, Saddam Hussein's burning of oil wells in the Gulf War.

E. Security of Energy and Natural Resources: Resources include water, sources of energy, land and minerals. Availability of adequate natural resources is important for a nation to develop its industry and economic power. Lack of resources is a serious challenge for Japan to overcome increase in its national power. In the Persian Gulf War of 1991, fought over economic issues, Iraq captured Kuwait in order to capture its oil wells, among other reasons. Water resources are subject to disputes between many nations, including the two nuclear powers, India and Pakistan. Nations attempt to attain energy and natural resource security by acquiring the desired resources by force, negotiation and commerce.

The interrelation between security, energy, natural resources, and their sustainability is increasingly acknowledged by the international community, as proven by the fact that energy is now one of the issues amidst the UN Sustainable Development Goals, as well as a cardinal issue for investment promotion policies at the national level.

F. Cyber Security: Recently, cyber security has begun to be viewed as a pressing national security issue. Electronic information systems are vital for maintaining national security of any state. Possible unauthorized access to the critical governmental infrastructures by state and non-state entities can create a serious threat and have a negative impact on political, economic and military security of a given nation.

Measures to Ensure National Security: These may include the following:

1. Using diplomacy to rally allies and isolate threats.
2. Marshalling economic power to facilitate or compel cooperation.
3. Maintaining effective armed forces.
4. Implementing civil defence and emergency preparedness measures (including anti-terrorism legislation).
5. Ensuring the resilience and redundancy of critical infrastructure.
6. Using intelligence services to detect and defeat or avoid threats and espionage, and to protect classified information.
7. Using counter intelligence services or secret police to protect the nation from internal threats.

National Security Council (NSC) of India: NSC is an executive government agency tasked with advising the Prime Minister's office on matters of national security and strategic interest. It was established by the Atal Bihari Vajpayee Government on November 19, 1998, with Brajesh Mishra as the first National Security Adviser. Prior to the formation of the NSC, these activities were overseen by the Principal Secretary to the Prime Minister.

Members of NSC include the following:

1. National Security Advisor (NSA).
2. Deputy National Security Advisor (DNSA).
3. Minister of Defence.
4. Minister of External Affairs.
5. Home Minister.
6. Finance Minister.

Other members may be invited to attend its monthly meetings, as and when required.

The three-tiered structure of the NSC comprises the Strategic Policy Group, the National Security Advisory Board and a Secretariat represented by the Joint Intelligence Committee (JIC).

A. Strategic Policy Group: The Strategic Policy Group is the first level of the three-tier structure of the National Security Council. It forms the nucleus of the decision-making apparatus of the NSC. This group consists of the following members:

1. Cabinet Secretary.
2. Chief of the Army Staff.
3. Chief of the Naval Staff.
4. Chief of the Air Staff.
5. Governor of the Reserve Bank of India (RBI).
6. Foreign Secretary.
7. Home Secretary.
8. Director of Intelligence Bureau.
9. Defence Secretary.
10. Secretary (Defence Production).
11. Finance Secretary.
12. Secretary (Revenue).

13. Secretary (Research) (i.e. the head of the Research and Analysis Wing).
14. Secretary of the Department of Atomic Energy.
15. Scientific Advisor to the Defence Minister.
16. Secretary of the Department of Space.
17. Chairman of the Joint Intelligence Committee (JIC).

The Strategic Policy Group undertakes the "Strategic Defence Review", a blueprint of short- and long-term security threats, as well as possible policy options on a priority basis.

B. National Security Advisory Board: The National Security Advisory Board consists of persons of eminence outside the Government with expertise in external security, strategic analysis, foreign affairs, defence, the armed forces, internal security, science and technology and economics. The board meets at least once a month, and more frequently as required. It provides a long-term prognosis and analysis to the NSC, and recommends solutions and address policy issues referred to it.

C. Joint Intelligence Committee (JIC): It analyses intelligence data from the Bureau, Research and the Directorates of Military, Naval and Air Intelligence. The JIC has its own Secretariat that works under the Cabinet Secretariat.

I take this opportunity to thank all the contributors to this volume for their respective scholarly articles which will surely add to the existing body of literature on India's defence and national security preparedness and concerns.

Kottayam **C. Vinodan**

1

India's Quest for Global Power Status in the 21st Century

Nalini Kant Jha

A recurring theme of Indian political and intellectual argument in the twentieth century was the desire to forge for India a place on the global stage. The end of the Cold War in 1990 brought about a sea change in the international system with the interplay of forces shaping international relations and the sources of power and influence in global polities witnessing sweeping changes thereafter. The post-Cold War world, therefore, demanded new strategies to facilitate India's quest for global power status.

Towards the end of the twentieth century, India's conduct of nuclear tests left nobody in doubt over India's ambitions of acquiring global power status in the 21st century. With the signing of the Indo-U.S. Agreement for civil nuclear cooperation as well as India's obtaining of the required waiver by the Nuclear Suppliers Group (NSG), the world has virtually recognized India as a nuclear power. But the international standing of India would rest on its economical and technological strength. Although India will always be strategically and commercially important because of its size, location and big consumer market, it will have to sustain its high economic growth rate to build its economic strength and bring about domestic stability if New Delhi wants to attain global power status in the world.

In the emerging world order in the 21st century, India has a remarkable opportunity to achieve an optimum global posture. But the challenges to be faced by India would be formidable, therefore it is necessary to ponder over what are the critical issues that have to be addressed and what kind of foreign policy would enable India to maintain its autonomy in international politics, secure its frontiers, cope with the challenges of cross-border terrorism, eradication of poverty, regaining and sustaining a growth rate of 8-10 percent per year so that it is able to achieve the status of a global power in the 21st century. Accordingly, this paper dwells upon the current world order; reasons for the emergence of India as a global power and the strategies to be adopted to achieve this goal as well as the challenges and hurdles, which New Delhi has to confront in this endeavour.

Emerging World Order

Though the United States is, and for the foreseeable future, will remain a pre-eminent power, no single nation can bear global burdens alone. In fact, the world today is such where the global agenda is being set by a constellation of nations including the United States, the European Union, Russia, China, Japan and India. The era when global politics was a zero-sum game is now decisively behind us. Leading nations, even when they compete, have inter-dependencies and linkages amongst themselves that they can ignore only at the cost of their own peril. Hence, the current international situation is characterized by the willingness of major nations to work together on issues and challenges where they perceive strong convergence.

A second aspect of the current global order is the changing paradigm of power. While the traditional notion of power was primarily based on military strength even though lip services were paid to other sources of power, the collapse of the Soviet Union, despite its vast military prowess, brought to the fore the significance of economic source of power. Hence, power is now judged by a much broader criteria that includes economic, technological, managerial and knowledge capabilities, in addition to military capabilities. The problems created by advanced industrialized countries of the West due to economic meltdown all the more manifested the significance of economy in influencing a country's status in global hierarchy of power.

Thirdly, as the global impact of economic meltdown in the U.S. and Europe demonstrated, globalization has thrown up challenges that are transnational and cross cutting in nature. They require coordinated responses. These challenges include not only economic crisis, but also terrorism, energy security, pandemics, natural disasters and environmental degradation.

Fourthly, the rise of religious fundamentalism along with the related problem of terrorism is posing a great threat to the peaceful economic growth of the world economy. Though the global community led by the U.S. has now stopped hailing terrorists as freedom fighters especially in South Asia, the problem is not yet abated. The way both the Bush as well as Obama administration have shown inclination towards negotiating a deal with the Taliban in Afghanistan, shows the limits of global war against terrorism.

Fifthly, there is now a widespread perception that non-state actors are an important factor to be reckoned with. They will have a particular relevance to many of the key challenges faced by the international community. Finally, an important aspect of the emerging world order is the growing clout of countries like India in several fields.

India's Growing Clout in the World

First and foremost, India growing at the rate of 8 percent per annum despite its recent slowdown has led to a very different attitude on the part of the leading countries of the world. An India of high growth rate creates new demands for goods, services and technologies that major global trading nations, like the U.S., cannot ignore. The experience of multinational companies already operating in India has been positive, as indeed has been their profitability. Those already in are expanding. Already it has an estimated 300 million plus middle class. India has clearly caught the world's attention and today it is invariably equated with China in terms of potential and possibilities.

The second significant component of India's growing power is the nuclear capability. The world cannot ignore India's 1.30 billion with nuclear weapons. This has made a compelling case for recognition of India's impeccable track record in non-proliferation of weapons of mass destruction and that of a responsible state with advanced nuclear technology. Accordingly, Washington persuaded the NSG—which was created after India's nuclear test in 1974 to checkmate India's nuclear ambition—to grant a special waiver to India to engage nuclear commerce with the world. Again, it was India's growing clout including the influence of the Americans of Indian origin that the U.S. could finally persuade its domestic critics to support U.S.-India nuclear agreement.

Thirdly, as a pluralist and secular democracy in a world where terrorist violence is on the rise, India has emerged as a model of stability, modernization and predictability that has begun to impact on international consciousness. To this, has been added a healthy respect for India's capabilities that have been steadily growing across the board. India has become a major interlocutor on key global challenges from environment and pandemics, to counter terrorism and disaster relief. The way an Indian navy-ship, Tabur, could destroy a pirate ship in the Gulf of Aden in November 2008, which no country was able to do earlier, has added another indicator of India's gradual rise as a major power shouldering global obligations regarding international security in the 21st century.

A fourth element of India's growing status in the world is its knowledge economy. The world is attaching importance to cooperation with a country like India that is producing a large number of engineers, software professionals, managers, technicians and doctors. There is recognition of the advancement made by India in the areas of science and technology, agriculture research, space, atomic energy, health or high technology. There is growing awareness of the demographic advantages of India. It has been argued that new service sector jobs in India along with China could exceed availability of similar skills in advanced economies.

The fifth point to be noted is that these developments are part and parcel of India's opening up to the world. The impact of India's integration with the global economy cannot be underestimated by the world in general and by major powers in particular. This is not just in terms of business, services or even connectivity, but the India Diaspora has established an enviable professional reputation in every sphere of socio-economic activity, an important factor that pushed the Bush administration towards concluding the nuclear deal with India. [1]

Sixthly, as an open society and as an open economy, the growth in India's capabilities has been welcomed by the world. India's spiritual record and its world view of *vasudhaiva kutumbakam* and its philosophy of yoga and vedanta should not leave apprehensions of any sort in anybody's mind, in the socio-cultural sphere, regarding India's rich cultural diversity. [2] India has always contributed towards addressing global challenges to the best of its ability, including the use of its military forces in UN peacekeeping missions. As Prof. Stephen Cohen has rightly pointed out, "India has long been counted among the have-nots. This situation is rapidly changing, which is what will make it such an interesting 'great' power for the next dozen years". [3]

The current world order and the trends likely to emerge in the near future demand certain strategies on the part of India that would facilitate its quest for global power status. While employing certain strategies, it is also certain that India would also face challenges and hurdles in attaining the goal of global power status. Hereunder, we would like to point out the following challenges that New Delhi is likely to face in attaining this cherished goal of a global power.

Managing Ties with the Major Powers

To begin with, managing relations with the United States

as well as with other major powers such as Russia, China, European Union and Japan requires a clear perspective and deft diplomacy. The one firm axiom at least for the next decade is that the US will remain the most decisive factor in shaping the contours of global politics and economy. Several other factors like economy, Indian Diaspora, counter-terrorism and China are bringing the two largest democracies together. With the successful conclusion of U.S.-India nuclear deal, the second phase of the Next Stage in Strategic Partnership with the U.S. has been successfully completed. Still there are issues that have to be addressed: Indo-U.S. defence cooperation has to graduate from military exchanges and expensive joint exercises to actual cooperation in weapons supplies and technology transfer. Both countries have to harmonize their interests where they intersect in Asia and in other spheres to establish a credible Indo-U.S. strategic partnership.

U.S. apart, India also has to balance its relationship with China that is emerging as a new super power of the world. After a tentative rapprochement that began at the end of the Cold War and a brief chill in bilateral relations following India's nuclear tests, India and China are today in the process of building an expansive relationship. Bilateral trade between the two countries is booming leading to an explosive mutual interaction between the people of the two countries. This does not mean that the sources of competition between New Delhi and Beijing have dried up; the long-standing border dispute is causing tension between the two nations, particularly regarding the Chinese incursions in the North-East. However, India has to build on areas of common interest with China and avoid a confrontation for which it is not prepared.

The relationship between these two Asian giants will, of course, is overshadowed by the presence of the U.S. in Asia. Some analysts speak of a triangular relationship emerging between the U.S., India and China and some talk of a trilateral relationship between India, Russia and China. Though India still enjoys good relations with Russia, it cannot take Russia for granted on the basis of its relations with the erstwhile USSR nor can it ignore Russia for it has all the makings of becoming another super power of the world in the future. This has given rise to some creative suggestions such as India being well-placed to be a "bridging power", [4] enjoying harmonious relations with the U.S., Russia, China and the EU.

Such a suggestion not only implies that the major global powers are willing to be "bridged", but also that India has the capabilities to serve as a "bridge". Moreover, the period of stable major power relations is rapidly coming to an end. Soon difficult choices have to be made and Indian policymakers should have enough self-confidence to make those decisions even when they go against their long-held predilections. But if the foreign policy lacks intellectual and strategic coherence then it will ensure that India, forever, remains poised on the threshold of great-power status, not quite ready to cross over.

Repairing Bridges of Friendship with South and South-East Asian Neighbours

Nearer home, India has to resolve or at least manage its troubled relationship with its immediate neighbours in South Asia. For decades, India's relations with these neighbours, especially Pakistan and Bangladesh, have been burdened by the bitter legacy of partition. However, India is actively negotiating the difficult issue of Jammu and Kashmir with Pakistan despite the enduring threat of cross-border terrorism. It is high time Prime Minister Manmohan Singh must find time to visit Pakistan and respond to the positive signals coming from the civilian government in that country. He must bypass bureaucratic hurdles and make political move to repair India-Pakistan relationship as done by his predecessor, Atal Behari Vajpayee.

Looking beyond Pakistan, India has recognized the urgency of promoting regional economic integration. New Delhi is prepared to offer unilateral economic concessions to its neighbours in an effort to lift all the countries in South

Asia. The idea of a peaceful periphery and the need to reintegrate the subcontinent within a single economic-zone should surely emerge at the top of India's regional agenda. At the same time, the problem of ethnic conflict in Sri Lanka, which has repercussions on India's domestic politics, is yet to be resolved. New Delhi has to build up a strong relationship with New Nepal. Hence, India has to deliberate upon how and to what extent it has been able to move towards addressing difficult issues with its neighbours and how the areas of disagreement could be minimized and agenda of cooperation could be expanded, as without friendly neighbours, India cannot concentrate on socio-economic development.

Domestic turmoil in the countries of South Asia has complicated the task. India has to strive to bring about stability in these countries and build up interdependence that not only integrates economies, but also creates vested interest in each other's prosperity and stability and it should seek to find out ways as to how to convince our neighbours that 'India is an opportunity and not a threat for them' and not an interventionist and a 'Big Brother' in the South Asian region.

Beyond South Asia, India has been making a strong bid to reverse its relative decline in the Indian Ocean and re-establish its economic and political relevance in Southeast Asia.

With the launch of the 'Look East Policy' in 1990's, India has established close cooperation with the Southeast Asian countries as well as with South Korea and Australia. Dramatic changes have been instituted through this new 'Look East Policy', such as the formation of the ASEAN (Association of Southeast Asian Nations) Regional Forum, BIMSTEC (Bangladesh, India, Myanmar, Sri Lanka and Thailand Economic Cooperation), BOBCOM (Bay of Bengal Community), and the Mekong-Ganga Initiative with Indo-China.

The challenge now is how to maintain the tempo of growing economic cooperation with these economic power houses. Similarly, ways have to be devised to ensure adequate external supplies of energy resources and raw materials from Central Asia and the Gulf. India has thus to develop a strong partnership with India's 'extended neighbourhood' [5] which includes Africa, the Middle East, the Persian Gulf, Central and inner Asia and the eastern parts of Asia.

Re-orienting NAM and Re-structuring the UN

As regards the Non-Aligned Movement (NAM), there is little disputing that its agendas of democratization of the world, disarmament, development and fight against decolonization are still relevant. Unfortunately, however, it has lost much of its momentum due to the end of the Cold War, as it was possible to play one super power against other and bargain something in favour of the Third World. Now when the major powers are competing with each other to gain favour from the sole surviving super power, the US, notwithstanding re-assertion of might by Russia in Georgia and the growing Chinese clout, India cannot afford to join any country or group of countries against the U.S., nor can it join with the U.S. to meet the Chinese threat to its security.

Under the circumstances, the best policy option available for the makers of India's foreign policy is to simultaneously improve its ties with all major powers of the world. In other words, the policy of non-alignment now has to be pursued in the form of multi-alignment. This can help New Delhi not only in gaining economic benefits, but also in maintaining its autonomy in world politics, which has been one of the most fundamental goals of Indian foreign policy ever since its Independence.

On the other hand, any talk of mythical Third World unity is not going to serve India's national interests. New Delhi must not forget that even during the hey days of NAM, hardly any Third World country supported India in the UN General Assembly during India-Pakistan war of 1971 despite India's constant advocacy of the cause of the Third World. India must, of course, coordinate her policy formulation with like-minded countries of the developing world, including China, in the course of negations concerning trade and environmental preservation with industrialized countries of the West. This cooperation must however be issue-based and without burning bridges of friendship with the rich countries. Reverting to old rhetoric of Third World unity appears to be out dated in the new century.

Besides, India has to press for the reforms of the United Nations so that it reflects the realities of today's world and not of 1945. Therefore, India is seeking for the reform of the U.N. Security Council and has sought a permanent seat for itself. Having garnered the support of Russia, Britain and France, India has to devise a strategy as to how it could attain a permanent seat in the U.N. Security Council in a reformed U.N. on the basis of its size, population, balanced regional representation, size of economy and contribution to peace-keeping and security.

Maintaining Minimum Nuclear Credible Deterrence

India has declared its policy of 'no first use' of nuclear weapons in case of a conflict and stands for genuine arms disarmament in the world, but realpolitik demands that it should continue with its nuclear weaponisation programme till it establishes a minimum credible nuclear deterrence, which could successfully counter the threats posed not only by Pakistan, but also by China.

The draft nuclear doctrine of the National Security Advisory Board (NSAB) headed by an eminent strategic expert, K. Subrahmanyam released on August 17, 1999 provides a broad framework for the development, deployment and employment of India's nuclear forces. It has proposed a credible, minimum nuclear deterrent retaliatory capability, consisting of sufficient, survivable and operationally prepared nuclear forces with the necessary support of an effective intelligence and early warning system. It has called for a triad consisting of bombers, land-based ballistic missiles and ballistic missiles launched from submarines. Such a triad is expected to constitute a "minimum and credible" deterrent against nuclear attack on Indian cities by India's main adversaries—Pakistan and China.

But, since the present Indian capabilities are limited, the triad will take many years to materialize. Inherent in the doctrine is the advocacy of a 'no first use' policy. This suggests that retaliation against a nuclear attack will be the preferred policy and not an offensive posture of the kind presently favoured by the U.S., Russia, France and the UK. Though Islamabad has recently come out with a 'no first use policy, Pakistan is yet to come out with a clear and concrete doctrine in this regard. It is, however, a welcome announcement by the Zardari government of Pakistan and New Delhi must initiate a dialogue with Islamabad to come out with a joint declaration on this issue.

In this context, it is relevant to discuss another distinctive feature of the proposed nuclear doctrine that is rejection of war fighting. Although often presented as complementary, there is a fundamental difference between strategies of nuclear deterrence and nuclear war fighting. For nuclear deterrence, it is not necessary that warheads should be matched with warheads and missiles with missiles. A modest sufficiency is enough. For nuclear war fighting, however, there is always a quest for nuclear superiority: more accurate delivery systems are also needed to destroy a large number of military targets. Nuclear deterrence threatens only punishment while the objective of nuclear war fighting is victory.

India claimed that the five nuclear weapons tests at Pokharan in May 1998 have provided enough data to its scientists and engineers to be able to conduct computer simulated sub-critical experiments (SCEs) at the laboratory not in the field. Such a view has not been shared by many who have favoured conducting further nuclear tests. From the scientific point of view, "a survivable nuclear deterrent" envisaged in the proposed nuclear doctrine could not be achieved without further testing. Indian nuclear weaponisation should include the development and testing of a neutron bomb because it is more efficient in weight and total energy production. One must not forget that it has taken the United States and Russia thousands of nuclear tests to arrive at SCEs. In any case, laboratory tests and computer simulations cannot provide complete reliability. India has to conduct many more tests to improve the warhead designs and maximize the yield to weight (Y/W) ratio as to reduce the payload on the missile.

Nuclear India has to build intercontinental ballistic missiles (ICBMs) because immunity from high tech aggression can come only if a country has the capability to hit the homeland of the attacking forces. If India is to gain true strategic autonomy, free itself from external pressure and be a global player, it will have to develop and deploy ICBMs, the symbols of power and punishment in international relations. India has successfully tested different types of missiles under its Integrated Missiles Development Programme (IMDP), but it has to ensure that its missiles use solid fuel instead of liquid fuel in order to ensure strategic superiority over its potential military adversaries.

Modernization of Armed Forces

India has to go in for a rapid military modernization of the Indian armed forces reversing the trend of decline in defence spending during the economic squeeze of the 1990s. India has to expedite the decision-making process, which has traditionally been slow, in the purchase of new weapons and which has become even worse in recent years thanks to the unending corruption scandals in defence acquisition. No country can aspire to become a great power without being a strong military power, therefore it has to dwell upon the steps required to be taken by the Indian government to upgrade its military might keeping in view of the security demands of today's world.

To enhance and modernize the military prowess, the annual defence budget should be placed at 3.5 percent of the

GDP for the next ten years. India's military budget is about one-sixth of Japan's and one-fourth of China's. Among the large nations, India has one of the lowest defence expenditure, whether calculated as a percentage of GDP or of overall national budget or as per capita spending. To heighten the stakes of foreign companies in India, the FDI limits in India have to be increased to 49 percent from the existing 26 percent. To hasten the emergence of India as the leading Asian defence research and manufacturing hub, India has to induct the Indian private sector to take up manufacturing of aircraft, warships, missiles etc. either individually, or in joint ventures with the multinationals. The deteriorating standards of the military, both in terms of human resources and equipment, are required to be reversed. In fact, the increasing security threats dictate that the military power apart from being lean and mean should be enhanced without any further delay.

There is no instance in history of a state becoming wealthy without military power or security. Politics generally triumphs over economics and because of its centrality to international relations, military power aids in the pursuit of relative economic advantage. [6]

Maintaining High Economic Growth

India will have to ensure that through proper global economic diplomacy, it is able to sustain a high growth rate of 8-10 percent in the coming years. It has been suggested that India is likely to overtake most European economies and Japan in size within the two decades and could become larger than the U.S. economy by 2050 and if not, it would be among the three largest economies of the world besides, the U.S. and China. Economic diplomacy could help in establishing the competitive advantage of India, because of its knowledge-based economy, in addition to its traditional comparative advantage. As its economy is based primarily on its domestic sector than on its external sector, therefore it is in a better position to deal with situations like the meltdown in the international financial markets etc.

Beyond GDP and growth rates, we need to look at a state's ability to access resources and its ability to use these efficiently. No military power can sustain its power without being a strong economic power. Therefore, it has to deliberate upon the steps to be taken to make full use of its technological, knowledge and skilled power to attain the goal of a global economic power.

An energetic economic diplomacy founded on a closer harmonization of foreign, commerce and economic policies can significantly aid the promotion of Indian interests. There is need for greater Indian involvement with the World Trade Organization (WTO) and the regional trading blocs. India needs to lay greater emphasis on economic issues in its foreign policy. While Indian statecraft should emphasize the attraction of the domestic market to foreign investors, sharply increased exports are crucial to accelerating India's growth rate and to providing the economic underpinnings for the long-term development of Indian military power. [7]

Challenges of Globalization and Managing Critical Issues

At the same time, India will have to persuade the major powers to fulfil promises and implement declarations made by them at the World Trade Organization (WTO). It is in this context that the set of challenges posed by the problems of globalization and managing certain critical issues comes in. Indeed, restructuring of the world economic order on the basis of WTO replacing the previous regimes of GATT and UNCTAD is one of the real challenges that India, along with other significant international actors, have to address. Similarly, addressing critical and interrelated issues such as food, water, energy, and environment, etc., are crucial for India's future.

Since India's energy dependence is likely to increase dramatically in the years to come, therefore a serious examination of India's energy security determinants is crucial.

Coal is the main component of India's energy consumption and production. Therefore, it has to look for alternative sources of renewable energy, though the signing of the Indo-U.S. civilian nuclear energy deal has been a significant step towards enhancing its energy resources. However, oil demand and supply will almost quadruple during the period between 1990 and 2020. [8]

Conclusion

For India to achieve the status of a global power, it has to find ways to exploiting the international system, as it exists. It will have to deliberate upon how to develop a national vision based on values and interests: one that could be realized through specific policies and institutions. It will have to think of ways to marshal the resources, at hand, in a manner that helps it to achieve the goal of global power status so that it is able to shatter the myth that India is always destined to be emerging but never actually arriving. [9]

Above all, the political community and intellectuals will have to develop a broad consensus about what constitutes India's national interest and how to preserve that. As the acrimonious debate on India-U.S. nuclear deal showed tremendous conflict about component of India's national interests. Indeed, the dynamics of socio-political and economic dilemmas confronting us today have eroded and diluted national consensus on vital issues of India's concern along with her sense of self, which acted as a source of our strength for the first two decades or so after Independence. Hence, it is necessary to develop a consensus about India's national interests to provide a meaningful framework for guiding the foreign policy of the country.

It is clear that today, Indian policy stands divided on fundamental foreign policy choices facing the nation. What Walter Lipmann wrote for U.S. foreign policy in 1943 applies equally to the Indian landscape of today. He had warned that the divisive partisanship that prevents the finding of a settled and generally accepted foreign policy is a grave threat to the nation. For when a people is divided within itself about the conduct of its foreign relations, it is unable to agree on the determination of its true interest. It is unable to prepare adequately for war or to safeguard successfully its peace. [10]

At the same time India has to ensure its domestic stability so that the disruptive forces of caste, religion and region along with Naxalism and terrorism do not create serious hindrances in attaining the cherished goal of becoming a global power. India has to remember that it has repeatedly fallen prey to marauding foreign forces. Internal disunity, sustained by an oppressively hierarchical social structure and rapacious power play, has remained its principal affliction.

Endnotes

1. For role of the Americans of Indian origin in bridging India-U.S. divide, see Nalini Kant Jha, "Americans of Indian Origin: Bridging the Gulf between Two Democracies", in Sarva Daman Singh and Mahavir Singh (eds.), 'Indians Abroad', Kolkata: Maulana Abul Kalam Azad Institute of Asian Studies, 2003, pp. 48-65.
2. See, for details, Nalini Kant Jha, "Cultural and Philosophical Roots of India's Foreign Policy", *International Studies,* New Delhi, Vol. 26, No. 1, January-March 1989, pp. 45-61.
3. Stephen P. Cohen, "India: An Emerging Power", Washington DC: Brookings, 2001, p. 35.
4. Sunil Khilnani, "India as a Bridging Power", in 'India as a New Global Leader', London: Foreign Policy Centre, 2005, p. 9.
5. C. Raja Mohan, "Indian Foreign Policy", *World Focus,* New Delhi, November-December 2007, p. 392.
6. Brahma Chellany, "Securing India's Future in the New Millennium", New Delhi, 1999, pp. 529-531.
7. Ibid., pp. 591-592.
8. "Energy Data Directory and Yearbook", Tata Energy Research Institute, 1998/1999.
9. Cohen, n. 1, p. 2.
10. Walter Lipmann, "U.S. Foreign Policy", New York, 1943, pp. 2-3.

2

Redefining India's Maritime Future

P.V. Rao

India is redefining her maritime destiny. There is definitely a sea-driven approach to major policy regimes like security, trade, resource mobilization, energy, infrastructure, transportation, tourism and many others. The rapid transformation in India's maritime thinking is mainly inspired by the twin shifts in the country's policy goals: security and economy. Fundamental change in the Asian security environment triggered by the collapse of the Cold War order, and advent of a market-led economy are the two key macro factors that compelled peninsular India to take seriously the Indian Ocean around her. Policy framers are drafting new visionary blueprints and policy frameworks to build a new maritime India. Concurrently, new policy instruments and mechanisms of policy execution are being devised. A major element in such transition is the involvement of private sector—native and foreign—in the maritime development of India. Building India's maritime power is the national objective.

'Maritime power' is a holistic concept into which the different variables of the sea, useful for the national welfare are capsuled. Maritime power is the sum total of sea-borne endowments which can be availed for national welfare of a coastal country. It should, however, be clarified that maritime power and naval power are not synonymous. Naval power denotes military power of a country's naval defence force. Building military capabilities to ensure maritime security of a littoral state, deter an adversary or hypothetical adversary, combat non-conventional threats from the sea (piracy, terrorism, arms/drugs trafficking, etc.; also called asymmetrical threats) are among the major purposes for which a coastal state like India would strengthen its naval power. Of course, an ambitious maritime power like India which wants to play an active role in global or regional politics empowers its naval force with advanced weaponry like carrier battle groups and aircraft carriers like the recently inducted INS *Vikramaditya* into the Indian Navy.

Therefore, what needs to be understood is that naval power is not the equivalent of maritime power. Naval power is a component of the military power. The tendency to equate both the terms need not be blamed on anyone because a layman is not expected to know about the subtle semantic distinctions. Moreover, since the navy enjoys visibility in comparison with other attributes of maritime power, one is apt to equate one with the other.

If naval power is not the same as maritime power, it is necessary to know what the latter implies. Leveraging sea resources for national good is maritime power. Sea is a depository of innumerable, perhaps inexhaustible properties. Taking advantage of them for national good is empowerment of a nation's power. As the *Indian Maritime Doctrine 2009* defines, "maritime power is the ability of a nation to use the seas to safeguard and progress its national interests. As such it is a pillar of national security policy and is a key to enabler in the formulation and implementation of viable national and military strategies". [1] National security and maritime power capacity building are closely intertwined.

Translating this ideal into actual is ridden with many constraints, most of important of them being budgetary and technological capacity. For, maritime power, among other attributes, involves modernizing port infrastructure and ship building; enhancement of sea-borne trade and transportation; use and conservation of living marine resources like fisheries; promotion of maritime domain awareness (MDA) and capacity building; exploration and utilization of seabed and subsoil mineral properties, and above all securing nation's sovereign maritime jurisdictions and wealth from foreign threats. But the crucial prerequisite for availing marine properties is political will. Indian government is generally criticized for the lack of political resole and direction to leverage marine wealth for nation's prosperity. However, for a variety of reasons and a few mentioned above, India is steadily realizing the importance of sea to national wealth.

There surely is national awareness in India about applying the marine endowments and hence building India's maritime power. Former chief of Indian Navy Admiral Arun Prakash, complaining about the lack of a cohesive governmental action to tap the sea resources in service of the nation, records his discomfiture in the following lines, "A comprehensive proposal for the constitution of a multi-disciplinary 'Maritime Commission' was mooted a few years ago by the Naval Headquarters, but ran into rough weather and finally foundered on the rocks of inter-Ministerial insecurity and rivalry. A nation such as ours urgently needs to evolve an overarching maritime policy and create a central agency to monitor its implementation". [2] In any case, it cannot be denied that today India is rather eagerly embarking upon building the country's maritime power, a concept which hardly two decades ago was unheard in the lexicon of the country's policy choices. What follows is a brief analysis of India's recent policy efforts to develop some of the key maritime attributes in order to promote a strong maritime India.

Maritime Security

The most familiar refrain in the commentaries on the Indian maritime policy is that the country had neglected the sea for a long time. It is argued that despite the fact that peninsular India is critically located across the key routes of the world linking the Pacific in the east with the Euro-Atlantic world through the Red Sea-Suez Canal passage in the west, Indian policy makers did not give adequate attention to formulate long-term policies aimed at securing the country's maritime interests. Sea is an extremely rich source of resources which the mankind can avail itself for its welfare. But a great deal of financial and technical investment is required to explore and exploit the maritime wealth for the good of a nation.

It is generally believed that the sea demands more attention from security point of view in the sense that the coastal and national security of a country like India can be threatened from sea and therefore adequate security measures should be designed to meet such contingencies. It is true that national security could be captive to maritime attacks as India had been attacked from the sea beginning with the Portuguese followed by other European imperial powers. What India's reputed Indian maritime historian K.M. Panikkar calls the beginning of the Vasco de Gama era in the Indian history, in effect the colonisation of India by European powers by sea. Historically, the argument runs that India had neglected the importance of sea to the national security as the security planners primarily focused on continental security, protecting Indian borders from attacks from the north. In plain language, army and air force gain more from the defence budget, not the Indian navy which traditionally received Cinderella treatment—least preferred and most neglected defence service.

Naval pundits continue to complain that the navy continues to be a less preferred security force despite the fact that in recent years, threat to India is more from the sea like the Mumbai terrorist attack, called 26/11. Former chief of Indian Navy Admiral Arun Prakash, an ardent advocate of a strong navy for India, expresses his displeasure about the neglect of the navy by the government in the following language, "India has neither acknowledged her role as a pre-eminent maritime entity in the Indian Ocean, nor done enough to shoulder the concomitant regional responsibilities. Consequently, *'Maritime India'* may present a conundrum to the citizens of a nation which has remained hostage to a continental mind set for centuries". [3]

Notwithstanding the complaints about the neglect of

maritime threats to national security, in recent years, Indian government has been paying greater attention to the building of strong naval forces. From a meagre 8-10 percent budgetary contribution to the navy out of the total annual defence budget in the previous decades, today the same has escalated to 18 percent. There is in fact a conscious realization by the Indian defence planners that a strong navy is the need of the hour if India has to attain the status of an Asian great power capable of playing active role in the regional balance of power politics. China is *the* major reason for bolstering the Indian naval military force and power projection capabilities to contain the Chinese rapid involvement in the Indian Ocean affairs and its so-called string of pearls strategy.

Therefore, Indian navy had published a series of maritime doctrines beginning with its first doctrine in 2004, followed by others in quick succession. Cumulatively, all these official doctrines had drawn the blue prints for a building a new maritime India. Henceforth, in the coming decades of the 21st century, India should be able to assert her strategic importance in the IO, reap the economic benefits of the seas, secure the energy supplies to the country, protect the crucial sealines of communications (SLOCs), and above all, counter extra-regional threats to India's maritime security—China in particular. The emphasis is on developing a strong Indian navy which can attain most of the objectives stated in the visionary doctrines.

The *Maritime Military Strategy* (2007) pronounces that whatever happens in the IO region can affect India's national security. Therefore, "our area of operations is extremely large" which is divided into two broad layers: primary and secondary areas. Primary area will cover the Arabian Sea and Bay of Bengal along with their island territories and littoral reaches; all major IOR choke points viz. Strait of Malacca, Gulf of Hormuz, Strait of Babel-el-Mandeb and the Cape of Good Hope; Persian Gulf; and, all principal ISLs (international sealanes) crossing the IOR. IN's secondary areas of coverage extend to the Southern Indian Ocean, Red Sea, South China

Sea and East Pacific region.

Practically, the entire Indian Ocean Region (IOR) should be under the domineering influence of the IN. Time framed for fifteen years, *Military Strategy* envisages building enough maritime capabilities to deter a hostile IO littoral power and raise the threshold against hostile extra-regional powers with inimical intentions. In this context, the sea-based leg of the nuclear triad is "a critical enabler for the nuclear doctrine". [4] *Military Strategy* sums up that its mission is to provide the rationale for the 'resurgence' of India's maritime military power, a deterrent strategy with 'offensive undertones'.

Maritime Infrastructure

Connectivity has become an important precondition of global economic integration. If economic integration in its broadest terms means increasing the trade and investment linkages between the nations, physical infrastructural facilities including road, rail and shipping networks, warehouses, cargo handling facilities, border posts, etc. are crucial for the countries engaged in economics of growth strategies. Briefly, connecting with the trade partners is the key to growth. To quote from the research report on maritime connectivity by RIS, the Delhi-based premier research centre on India's foreign economic policy, "Maritime transportation helps strengthen the economic integration—global or otherwise. Not only it plays an important role in the development of an economy, performance and efficiency of ports and shipping positively contribute to the growth of trade and vice versa". [5]

While the developed industrialised countries have over the centuries, beginning with the Industrial Revolution, have laid down stronger foundations of transport networks and kept them upgraded as their technological progress advanced, developing country like India suffers from poor maritime and shipping facilities which are the lifelines of growing economic linkages. As the Asian economies of the late twentieth century began growing fast, the imperative need for a well structured transport and communication networks linking the trading partners has been acutely realized. Being a rapidly growing economy which is fast integrating its trade transactions with the other growth destinations in the Asia-Pacific and other regions, for India it is imperative to take urgent measures to develop her maritime infrastructure.

India is a late entrant into the Asian globalizing process. She was of course the major partner in the pre-colonial Asian economy. It is a well recorded fact that India and China of the pre-European era together accounted for two-third of the global economic output and exchange. India's 'Look East Policy' had ushered the new era of integrating the Indian economy with the growth centres of Asia, and beyond. In a rather historical sense, India is trying to regain her past role in Asia. But what she needs is stronger land and sea connectivities to facilitate rapid economic interaction with her economic partners.

It is known that quite a few economic instrumentalities between India and the Asian countries in the East are in place. It may be recognized that India is a key link in the *Arc of Prosperity* of the fast growing chain of Asia-Pacific growth poles like China, Japan, ASEAN group, South Korea and Japan. But it should also be realized that compared to the shipping infrastructure of these countries, India is a weak link. Larger India-bound merchant ships have to download their cargo at Singapore or Colombo harbours, to be ferried to the Indian coast.

Maritime infrastructure is a key prerequisite of maritime power. It involves the development of various structural components which can help a nation to constructively reap the benefits offered by the ocean. If the ocean is a vast domain of resources, the coastal areas require adequate means and mechanisms of transporting cargo, oil and other products. Sea connects land to the other parts of world in several ways. India's destiny is closely linked to the Indian Ocean which throughout the centuries beginning with the Indus Valley civilization has been a great means of connecting India to countries in Asia and Africa, even beyond into the Pacific Ocean. Growth-led Indian economy today is actively engaged in building economic partnerships with major economies like China, Japan, South Korea and all other major economic destinations in Europe, American continents and the Pacific Rim states.

Unless the littoral country is well equipped with an efficient system of maritime transportation, trade does not grow. India is a heavily sea-borne country with about 95 percent of her international trade carried through sea lanes of communication (SLOCs), the sea routes. However, till recently, despite heavier economic stakes involved, India still lacks efficient maritime infrastructure—ports capable of handling bulk cargo, handling incoming and outgoing cargo quickly without huge delays, linking internal land and river routes to the ports, terminals and warehouses to store perishable items like fish, fruits and vegetables. Indian ports and shipping services are not efficient and advanced to meet the ever growing demands of seaborne trade.

Realising the urgent need for efficient shipping infrastructure, Indian government had taken a major policy decision to improve the country's port structure. Hence, the NDA government led by Atal Behari Vajpayee introduced an ambitious project called *Sagarmala.* Under this ambitious plan, India proposed to build large number of ports, almost one port on an average for every seventy five kilometres on the Indian coastline. It involved building new major or minor ports depending upon the shipping needs and logistics, or upgrading and modernizing an existing port. Currently, India has 212 sea ports of which 13 are major ports and 200 are non-major ones.

Several projects under the *Sagarmala* scheme have been taken up on the country's eastern and western coasts. Gujarat is a heavily concentrated state on the western coast which has undertaken the largest number of ports and hence stands out as having the largest number of well advanced ports in the country. Not only public sector but even private sector is heavily involved in the development of Gujarat's shipping infrastructure involving some of the leading Indian corporate bodies like the Reliance and Adani groups. On the east coast of Andhra Pradesh, which has the second longest coastline next to Gujarat and Tamil Nadu, is also witnessing brisk port construction projects such as in Krishnapatnam and Ennore and the Sethusamudram canal project.

Apart from the traditional ports, modern shipping is serviced by container and transhipment hubs. Globally, maritime trade is moving away from the vessel-led shipping to container carriers. Unfortunately, India lags behind the global movement toward container and transhipment facilities. Indian government therefore has initiated steps to build container and transhipment infrastructure in recent years. The International Container Transhipment Terminal (ICTT) at Valarpadem, Kochi is country's first transhipment terminal undertaken in 2011. The ICTT is being partnered by Dubai Port World (DPW). Once completed, this ambitious project is expected to lubricate economic growth across south India.

Inaugurating the ICTT, Prime Minister Manmohan Singh said, "The terminal is the centre-piece of a comprehensive plan to develop Kochi as an economic and logistical hub of the region". He said that because of the absence of a global hub port and the lack of transhipment facilities, about sixty percent of India's export and import containers were transhipped through outside ports such as Singapore and Colombo, involving an additional cost of "US$ 300 per container and an extra 7-10 days time. With the new facility, Indian exporters can now access maritime container vessels". [6]

Growing India is also establishing connectivities with other major ports and trading hubs of Asia in recent years. One such recent example is the feeder service between India and Bangladesh which commenced in March 2016. This service will connect Indian ports of Kolkata, Paradip, Vizag, Kakinada, Krrishnapatnam and Chennai with the Bangladesh ports of Ashuganj, Chittagong, Khulna and Mongla. [7] Similarly, some of the major ports like Ennore promise Indian maritime connectivity with Southeast Asian ports like the Sittawe port of Myanamr which is built by India. Vizag port is set to become a transhipment port linking its regular cargo service to Colombo, Dubai, Pangaon, and Singapore. It is also "set to emerge as EXIM gateway for Nepal, with the Himalayan country signing agreement with India in February 2016". [8]

Energy Security

Securing uninterrupted oil supplies for a growing economy like India is an imperative. That India is an oil dependent country which imports above 70 percent of her energy requirements from abroad is a well-known fact. But, what is less known is the fact that India is keenly pursuing an aggressive 'energy diplomacy' from any global source including Africa, Australia, Central and Southeast Asia, Latin America, Russia and of course the traditional oil supplying region, West Asia. Indian government has drawn major energy security vision plans including the *Hydrocarbon Vision 2020* and *National Solar Mission* among others. Long-term energy agreements are signed with foreign countries and exclusive oil summits are held with oil rich regions. India-Africa Hydrocarbon Summit is one such major initiative.

Energy supplies were conventionally understood as the import of fossil fuels—crude oil and natural gas—from the regular and rich Arab sources. However, for a variety of reasons—competitive pressure, rising prices, political fluidity, climate change mandates—consuming countries are steadily moving toward alternative energy sources. This does not mean a complete shift away from the hydrocarbons, but an evident tendency to prefer non-conventional fuels like nuclear, solar, tidal, wind and bio-diesel. Hence, today, the noticeable trend is that the energy importing countries are simultaneously trying to explore the globally available sources of nuclear material and technologies as also the technologies of solar, tidal and bio-fuels. What needs to be understood therefore is that energy security is no more the craving for conventional supplies, but also the demand for unexplored non-fossil energy minerals and technologies. India is actively on the path of exploring every non-conventional source of energy within and outside the country.

Shipping safely the foreign oil supplies to India is ridden with serious security problems posed by pirates and maritime terrorists. Hence, national security and energy security are being synergized. Thus, energy security and SLOCs have become the sin qua non of maritime security. *Indian Maritime Doctrine* (2009) in recognition of such threats says that "overall naval development must be directly related to the support of our national interests and not just perceived threat. This includes India's seaborne trade, the safeguarding of our EEZ, and the growing offshore oil production". [9]

In the Annual Report (2001-02) of the Ministry of Defence (MoD), energy security finds mention in the section on 'maritime dimensions in Indian Ocean'. But it is the Group of Ministers (GoM, 2001) Report, the important official policy document on national security that places 'energy security' under the 'maritime security'. The relevant GoM section says, "India has a vital interest in the security and stability of the Sea-lanes of Communications (SLOC) in the Indian Ocean; our energy security is closely linked to maritime security". Naval officials have been frequently endorsing publicly this view and one such statement attributed to the Indian Navy Chief Admiral Suresh Mehta is, "Our area of operation is not just restricted to the Indian Ocean; we are also engaged in securing energy lines and sea lines of communications". [10]

Blue Economy

Blue economy is an emerging ocean-related development paradigm. It emphasizes use of ocean resources for the socio-economic development of coastal as well as non-coastal countries which have access to the ocean spheres. The difference between the common development approach, called 'brown economy', is that the latter exploits natural resources including the sea-borne to maximum the benefit for consumable, industrialization and exploitative purposes to meet the growing consumer desires of an economy, essentially the market-led economy of modern state. Blue Economy on the other hand represents the non-conventional approach to the application of sea-borne properties for development but with emphasis on conservation and sustainable development.

The Blue Economy movement is articulated by the coastal and island states which are strongly sensitive to the commercial practices of the modern states in their exploitation of ocean resources without caring for their ecological and sustainable effects. In a way this concept is a reaction to the uncontrolled drive on the ocean resource, the global commons, by the technologically advanced societies for their consumer-led economies. To quote the relevant part from the United Nations Conference on Sustainable Development held in 2012:

"Blue Economy conceptualises oceans as 'Development Spaces' where spatial planning integrates conservation, sustainable use, oil and mineral wealth extraction, bio-prospecting, sustainable energy production and marine transport. The Blue Economy breaks the mould of the business as usual "brown" development model where the oceans have been perceived as a means of free resource extraction and waste dumping; with costs externalised from economic calculations". [11]

The Blue Economy is modelled on the historic "Rio +20" United Nations Conference on Sustainable Development (UNCSD) held in Rio de Janeiro in 2012. The Rio Declaration emphasized two key themes which should guide development goals: 'sustainable development' and promotion of 'green economy' concept. It is the extension of eco-development model to the ocean resources.

India is trying to emulate the blue economy model.

Official India is steadily educating concerned marine agencies on the need to adopt blue economy strategies. For instance, India's Ministry of External Affairs (MEA) is hosting series of blue economy international conferences to advance the blue economy cause. India as a founder and active member of the IORA (Indian Ocean Rim Association), has conducted an IORA Dialogue on 'Prospects of Blue Economy in the Indian Ocean,' in August 2015 at Goa. Reportedly another such conference on the same theme is planned in 2016. In fact, the present NDA government has signed with island countries of IO, Mauritius and Seychelles, agreements on promotion of the blue economy. It is interesting to note that the President of India's address to the 16th Lok Sabha announced government's priority to establish a National Maritime Authority, an apex body to formulate and coordinate integrated development of India's marine resources.

In 2015, the Indian government approved the National Wind Energy Policy that seeks to promote and streamline the process of implementing offshore wind energy projects. India's Ministry of New and Renewable Energy, the nodal agency for wind energy promotion, is encouraging wind energy (a blue energy concept) projects in India's coastal states of Andhra Pradesh, Gujarat, Karnataka, Maharashtra and Tamil Nadu. These projects however reportedly are facing some problems of execution.

About 600 wind monitoring centres are established on the Indian coast, of which reportedly 140 are operational. Going by the experience of this blue energy wind power, it appears India has to invest more human and financial resources into the blue economy promotional projects. As an Indian official stated, "private sector participation needs to be encouraged in this sector". Suzlon Energy Ltd. is engaged in a 600 mw off-shore wind energy project on the coast of Gujarat, India's western state with largest coastline and as also the largest private sector-participated maritime state. In view of these policy initiatives, "much hope is pinned on efficient implementation of the wind energy policy since this could significantly help the country in attaining its target of 60 GW of installed wind capacity by 2020". [12]

Conclusion

Above analysis is about India's recent efforts to charter a maritime vision that befits the demands of the current century, the Asian Century, also often called the Maritime Century. There is an evident rise in maritime of consciousness in India and the gradual efforts to shape it into functional instruments. Compared to all the preceding ages, India as also the other maritime countries of Indian Ocean, are under pressure to take sea more seriously from not just security point of view, but also from maritime dimension. Current age, characterised by rapidly integrating economic forces on the one hand and endangered by trans-regional maritime threats on the other hand, is demanding greater seaward focus by coastal states.

Oceans are fast losing their geographical borders and distinctions. There surely is trans-oceanic integration of economies, transport networks, security networks and people. Symbolic of such integrating processes is the Japanese call for Confluence of Oceans; China's Maritime Silk Route; Indo-Pacific; Atlantic Indo-Pacific; and India's *Mousam.* All these maritime formulations identify India as a key factor. India faces opportunities and challenges as well from these apparently varying and substantively integrating trans-oceanic scenarios. To meet such contingencies, India therefore, has to strengthen her maritime power, a process not an easy one. But, fortunately India is evidently endeavouring towards that end.

Endnotes

1. "Indian Maritime Doctrine 2009", p. 10.
2. Adm. Arun Prakash, "From the Crow's Nest", Lancer, New Delhi, 2007, p. 76.
3. Adm. Arun Prakash, "A Vision of Maritime India 2020", *Indian Defence Review,* January-March 2007, p. 10.
4. "Freedom to Use the Seas: India's Maritime Military Strategy",

Integrated Headquarters, Ministry of Defence (Navy), New Delhi, 2007, p. 22.

5. Research and Information System for Developing Countries, "ASEAN-India Maritime Connectivity Report", New Delhi, 2014, p. 4.
6. *The Hindu*, February 12, 2011.
7. Ibid., March 25, 2016.
8. Ibid., April 10, 2016.
9. "Indian Maritime Doctrine 2009", Integrated Headquarters, Ministry of Defence, New Delhi, 2009, p. 22.
10. See, P.V. Rao, "Energy Security and Navy", *Journal of Indian Ocean Studies,* New Delhi, 2006, p. 5.
11. "The Future We Want", UNCSD, United Nations Conference on Sustainable Development, 2012.
12. Admiral Pradeep Chauhan, "The EEZ and India's Blue Economy", *Journal of Indian Ocean Studies*, Vol. 23, No. 3, December 2015, p. 325.

3

Indian Foreign Policy 'Modi'fied: From Non-alignment to Multi-vectored Alignment

Mohanan Bhaskaran Pillai

For the first time in the history of independent India, in 2014, a cultural nationalist party which considers secularism and pluralism of Indian National Congress as minority appeasement has come to power with a massive mandate. It was widely anticipated that in tune with its cultural nationalism, BJP government would come out with a distinct foreign policy framework abandoning the Nehruvian architecture. The question is whether such a complete departure from the Nehruvian architecture is visible in the foreign policy front during the last two years of the Modi government.

Many analysts have argued that in the aftermath of the demise of the bipolar world order, Indian foreign policy has become more realistic in its application and the new initiatives like the 'Look East Policy' and the economic reforms paved the way for the rise of India as one of the three or four great powers of the world. For instance, Devin Hagerty taking into account the emerging balance of power from a neo-realist perspective argued that India would emerge as a great economic and military power by 2020 (Hagerty, 2009).

According to Harsh V. Pant (2009, p. 12), four major influences have been shaping India's foreign policy since the end of Cold War viz., "changing global balance of power, the emerging global order, the challenge of global terrorism and India's pursuit of energy security'. It has been argued that the end of Cold War is really the beginning of the foreign policy of India as it was 'free from the structural constraints of a bipolar world order" (p. 3). He further writes that India has already moved away from the periphery of the international system to the centre-stage where India is one among the six members of the new global balance of power. Another assessment is that India is one among the fourth most important country in the present day international system. According to Goldman Sachs, the international investment banking corporation, India will emerge as the fourth most important economic and political power by 2040 (as quoted by Pant, 2009).

These kinds of assessment of India's power position is based on the premise that the idealist overtones of Nehruvian architecture of domestic and foreign policy has been replaced with a realist and pragmatic policy framework as a consequence of the demise of Cold War-based bipolar international system. Further, the trends and shifts in India's foreign policy are determined by the changes in the global balance of power. The policies of post-Cold War Indian governments' right from that of Narasimha Rao down to Manmohan Singh have been rated as pragmatic and realistic as narrated above. The moot question is whether the Modi government is a complete disconnect with the immediate past in the matter of economic and foreign policy?

Several analysts have expected that the advent of Modi would facilitate the emergence of a truly right wing foreign and domestic policy. For instance, Bharat Karnad has expected that the advent of Modi 'would root a liberal right wing Edmund Burke-ian type of conservatism in the country'. However, he is of the opinion that, "the BJP regime has not deviated an iota from the Congress government's pusillanimous approach and outlook. India continues to acquiesce in security schemes on terms dictated by extra-territorial powers, U.S. and China" (Karnad, 2016). Another perceptive analyst has written that on several occasions, Modi has acted like the Bull in China shop (Bhadrakumar, 2016).

Bhadrakumar has made this comment specifically in the

context of the Dharmasala Conference of Chinese dissidents. In another article, Bhadrakumar has pointed out that there is very little to show by Modi government as achievement in foreign policy front during the last two years. Prakash Karat has written that "the Bharat Mata which is hailed by the Hindutva forces will soon have to hold the stars and stripes in one hand while the other holds the *bhagwa jhanda*. Absent will be the tricolour" (Karat, 2016). Karat has pointed out that at a time when the RSS-BJP combine has been whipping up nationalist fervour and targeting the so-called antinational activities in the country, many of Modi government's domestic and foreign policy measures happened to be anti-national and detrimental to the national interest of the country.

In my opinion, the principal determinant of India's foreign policy is the international political economy. The economic pronouncements of Prime Minister Narendra Modi, like the 'Make in India' type, indicated that he would continue the reforms that was initiated in 1991 by the Congress government of Narasimha Rao, on a fast pace. In other words, Prime Minister Modi's policy statements have emitted strong signals of deepening further the integration of the Indian economy with the capitalism of "financialized, generalized, and globalized monopolies" (Amin, 2006).

The question is whether such a fast paced mode of integration with the global economy and the so-called muscular foreign policy could help India to achieve great power status, which has been a foreign policy objective of India right from the days of Nehru? In what way the foreign policy of India is being shaped in the context of fast paced integration of Indian economy with the global economy? Is there any visible shift in India's foreign policy in accordance with the cultural nationalism of BJP and the economic philosophy to which that party is wedded to?

Keeping in mind the above questions, this paper is arranged in five sections. The first section is a brief assessment of the political economy of neo-liberalism followed by an analysis of the trends and shifts in India's foreign policy. The third section discusses the trends and shifts in India's foreign policy. The fourth section tries to find out if any Modi doctrine has surfaced within the span of two years. The fifth section rediscovers 'strategic autonomy' as a fairly constant element in India's foreign and strategic policy framework followed by the concluding observations.

Global Political Economy: From Liberalism to Neo-liberalism

The Bretton Woods institutions that came into existence to manage the post-War international economic order developed fatigue from the beginning of the eighties of the last century. Some analysts have stated that the performance capabilities of Bretton Woods institutions started eroding right from the second half of the seventies. Since then, there had been a calculated move to bring to the fore the individualistic philosophy of Frederick Hayek, in the major centres of learning in the United States. The economists who got trained in such U.S. Universities—particularly Chicago—have been placed in key positions in the World Bank, IMF and the GATT, as well as in national governments in different countries including the third world.

Thus, a consent was constructed in favour of neo-liberal policies the world over. The Chicago boys, as they were fondly called, liberated the Bretton Woods trio from the domineering influence of Keynesianism, and were remodelled in accordance with Frederick Hayek's postulates of individual's freedom first and the economic ideas of Milton Friedman. The new international economic order thus emerged, controlled by the World Bank, IMF, WTO, Wall Street and the US treasury, and which advocated structural adjustment and free trade for the third world countries and protective measures for the Western economies. The Bank who administered structural adjustment pill to the third world economies advised the gradual withdrawal of subsidies for their early convalescing from the illness of mal-development and non-performance.

The revolution in the field of information and communication technology has emerged as a handy tool for controlling the third world economy and for transfer of wealth from the third world region to the global centres of monopoly capitalism. The third world economies were advised to replace import substitution industrialisation with industrialisation by invitation. In place of collective self-reliance, dependent growth became the new paradigm. Devaluing of national currencies, foreign direct investment, privatisation of public assets and similar measures have been promoted under the structural adjustment programmes. In this process, concepts like collective self-reliance, new international economic order (NIEO), South-South cooperation, which were so ardently advocated by Prime Minister Indira Gandhi and other third world leaders were unfairly consigned to oblivion.

The sole hegemonic power, which presides over and provides politico-military support to the new international political economy, constructed strategies for the control of the natural resources of the world. It is actually the extension of the Monroe Doctrine to the entire planet. The U.S. has developed strategies to have full control over Europe through NATO, to keep former republics of the Soviet Union as hot beds of tension, to keep Russia always in trouble, to balance China, to subordinate countries like India, Brazil and South Africa, to keep West Asia and Latin America as backyards of the U.S. and to plunder the natural resources of the African continent.

This political strategy to have control over the planet is intertwined with monopolistic control over science and technology in general and information technology in particular by the U.S. and its European allies. Moreover, the developed West has moved on to the stage of post-industrialisation and they are very much interested in relocating polluting industrial units to third world regions. This strategy has been integrated into the new production strategy of decentring. As a result of relocating manufacturing units to the third world regions, countries like India, China, and Brazil are now facing the problems associated with environmental externalities.

The above mentioned shift in the international political economy that started unfolding during the 1978-80 period, much ahead of the disintegration of Soviet Union and the collapse of East European regimes which was called the shift from 'Embedded Liberalism' to Neo-liberalism (Harvey, 2003), has stripped capitalism of its liberal façade, and, as a result, the welfare states in the West and the socialist pattern of governance as it was found in India and other third world countries paled into oblivion to pave the way for the thunderous entry of techno-capitalism which is dominated and guided by finance capital.

In the context of such a massive shift in international political economy, India confronted a situation where it had no other go but to introduce the structural adjustment programmes at the behest of the Fund-Bank combine under the leadership of Prime Minister Narasimha Rao and Finance Minister Manmohan Singh. The United Progressive Alliance (UPA) I and II governments under the premiership of Manmohan Singh further liberalised the economy and integrated it with the global economy. The non-Congress governments that came to power in-between, including that of A.B. Vajpayee, continued the same policy with minor changes here and there in the operational side. However, due to the constraints imposed by coalition politics and the pressure exerted by other social formations in general and leftist political parties in particular, full integration did not take place at the desired level.

At the same time, it has to be noted that there are attempts from the part of a few countries in the world to construct alternative institutions to the Fund-Bank combine. India is part of multilateral interactions with its membership in the four nation grouping called BRICS (Brazil, Russia, India, China and South Africa) to strengthen collective relationships. This grouping's political interaction could help to alter the shape of the international financial system and the global economy. One of the objectives of the grouping is democratization of international financial institutions. The joint declaration at the first summit meeting held in Russia focused on global food security. The BRICS countries supported the adoption of a wide range of mid- to long-term measures in order to provide for a solution to the issue of food security.

The BRICS Fortaleza Summit announced the establishment of the New Development Bank (NDB) with a US$ 50 billion subscribed capital and a Contingency Reserve Arrangement (CRA) of US$ 100 billion. These measures have the potentialities to alter the monopoly status and role of the Bretton Woods institutions.

According to Shyam Saran, "the emergence of an alternative source of financing with norms different from those followed by the established institutions will alter the global financial landscape irreversibly" (Saran, 2014). He has written further that "the BRICS initiatives were born out of mounting frustration among emerging countries that even a modest restructuring of the governing structures of the Bretton Woods institutions, to reflect their growing economic profile, was being resisted. The commitment made in 2010 at the G20 to enlarge their stake in the IMF remains unfulfilled while the restructuring of the World Bank is yet to be taken up" (Saran, 2014).

It is to be kept in mind that the U.S. has devised strategies to defeat the BRICS efforts. For instance, Ashton Carter has recently spelt out the five evolving major immediate challenges to the U.S. security interests. They are: "(i) countering the prospects of Russian aggression and coercion, (ii) managing historic change in the vital Asia-Pacific region, including China's rise, (iii) strengthening U.S.' deterrent and defence forces against North Korea, (iv) checking Iranian aggression and malign influence in the Gulf, and (v) accelerating the defeat of the Islamic State" (Bhadrakumar, 2016). Similarly, the ouster of Brazil President Roussef will definitely weaken the prospects of BRICS.

India's Foreign Policy Strategy: Trends and Shifts

India's foreign policy strategy right from the days of Independence has been built brick by brick on the nationalist desires and aspirations that got gradually crystallised during the course of the freedom movement. The objective of the foreign policy doctrine has been to carve out a niche for India among the league of the great powers of the world. The civilization legacy of India, size, culture, history, geography and, above all, domestic and international political economy influenced Nehru while crafting the non-aligned approach to India's foreign policy. The Hindu cultural ethos, Jainist, Buddhist thought systems formed the inner crest of Nehru's vision on India's foreign and strategic policy which received the supplementary nourishments from the Islam, Christianity and modern Western rationality and above all the ethos of representative democracy. Gandhi's pacifist approach, which is rooted in the teachings of Gita, Jainism and Buddhism, has also influenced Nehru.

The plural and secular democratic approach to foreign and strategic policy maintained unstinting faith in democratic institutions and international organizations in conflict transformations. The core values of this stream of thought are strategic autonomy and faith in regional and international organizations' ability to mitigate conflicts. The *mandala* concept of concentric circles as codified by Kautilyain *Arthasastra* had also influenced Nehru's views on non-alignment and its core value—the strategic autonomy.

Notwithstanding the shift in emphasis at the operational level in accordance with the changes in the domestic and international milieu, the Nehruvian architecture of non-alignment was followed by successive prime ministers of both Congress and non-Congress governments. It has to be underlined that non-alignment emphasised political and strategic autonomy along with a self-reliant growth path guided by the mixed economy policy framework without challenging the basic tenets of liberal capitalism, the international political economy of the post-War period. Nehru's attempt was to industrialise a dependent agrarian economy that was left behind by the retreating British colonialism with the support of borrowed technology and domestic capital. Since domestic capital was so fragile at that point of time, the Indian state had offered protection to the domestic capital from the possible onslaughts of international capital.

At the same time, Nehru emphasised the importance of the creation of a strong public sector for the economic growth and development of the country. Since he designed his populist national model of economic growth strategy and international engagement mechanism within the domain of liberal capitalism, Nehru and subsequently his daughter Indira Gandhi could not effectively tackle certain vestiges of colonialism effectively. This is evident from the fact that Congress party could not pay much attention to the redistribution of wealth, despite the rhetoric of socialism because of the active presence of certain structures inherited from the dependent agrarian economy of the past.

As a result, Nehru and the Indian National Congress did not take up seriously, the agrarian reforms to transform the inherited structures. Because of this, poverty continues as a major social evil in India even after sixty nine years from the date of attainment of freedom from colonial clutches. However, it is noteworthy that Nehru and Indira Gandhi very efficiently leveraged the flexibility of liberal capitalism and the bipolar division of international political order for promoting industrialisation of the country by import substituting strategies and tactics. The leverage of equidistance internationally and mixed economy platform domestically for economic growth prevented in a substantial way, the expansion of dependent peripheral capitalism despite the active presence of inherited structures from the colonial past.

The economic reforms initiated by Narasimha Rao government just in the aftermath of the crumbling down of the bipolar world order led to massive readjustment in India's foreign and strategic policy. For the first time since

Independence, India opened diplomatic relations with Israel and initiated the 'Look East Policy' with a noticeable strategic overtone. It is appropriate here to take cognizance of the offer of Condoleezza Rice, U.S. Secretary of State in Bush Jr. Administration, that the U.S. would facilitate India to attain the great power status on condition of abandoning the non-alignment and getting on the bandwagon with the U.S. India which always favoured to keep away great powers from the Indian Ocean is now not averse to the presence of the U.S. in the Indian Ocean region and quietly buried the concept of Indian Ocean a zone of peace.

Strategic partnership with the U.S. was taken to new heights by signing of the nuclear accord during Manmohan Singh's period. In the matter of relations with India's immediate neighbours in South Asia, Vajpayee and Manmohan Singh, while operating from within the framework of neo-liberalism, followed some kind of a middle path between Indira Gandhi's doctrine of 'hegemonic interventionism' and Gujral's doctrine of 'restraint magnanimity'.

As has been noted elsewhere, the economic reforms initiated by Narasimha Rao government just in the aftermath of the crumbling down of the bipolar world order led to massive readjustment in India's foreign policy strategy. Since then, economics has emerged as the powerful locomotive of foreign policy calculus. The demise of the bipolar world order and the liberalisation, privatisation and globalisation programmes in the economy prompted analysts to argue that India abandoned non-alignment once and for all as it had become obsolescent at the strategic juncture of the unipolar world order. The pro-U.S. academic lobby in India fervently argued and continues to argue that an alignment with the U.S. is the only viable strategy for India's economic redemption and appropriate placement in the hierarchy of the great powers. Of late, the pro-U.S. lobby has emerged more influential after the opening up of the branches of Brookings Institution and

Carnegie Endowment in New Delhi (Karnard, 2016).

On the other side, the strategic autonomy school argued that, in the contemporary global situation, India had to work for multi-alignment to maintain strategic autonomy. India embraced liberalisation, privatisation and globalisation (LPG) in the beginning of 1990s under the dual leadership of Narasimha Rao as Prime Minster and Manmohan Singh as the Finance Minister. It was taken forward by successive prime ministers. In a phased manner, privatisation and liberalisation of the economy had been taken forward by Narasimha Rao's Government and UPA I and II coalitions of Prime Minister Manmohan Singh and the non-Congress governments that came to power during the Congress interregnum.

Acceptance of the international trade regime under the WTO umbrella, export-oriented industrialisation, FDI and devaluing of the currency quite often fulfilled the basic minimum qualification for graduating as a junior partner into the economic order of monopoly capitalism. In this process, the Nehruvian framework of mixed economy and Indira Gandhi's passion for a new international economic order through South-South cooperation had been thrown into the Arabian Sea and the Bay of Bengal respectively by successive leaderships of the Congress party from the Nehru dynasty itself. A shift in India's foreign policy was discernible with the announcement of the 'Look East Policy' and a closer partnership with the U.S. and the opening up of full diplomatic relations with Israel.

These adjustments in the making of foreign policy were a result of the shift in international political economy from *embedded liberalism* to neo-liberalism. Interpreting these adjustments in India's foreign policy as abandonment of non-alignment and getting onto the bandwagon with the U.S. is without taking into account the dynamics of underlying economic forces. So is the argument of 'shift from non-alignment to multi-alignment'. It was actually the subordination of the Indian economy to the manipulation of international capital by the Indian comprador class.

The Modi Doctrine

For the first time in the history of independent India, a non-Congress party that believes in Hindu cultural nationalism has come to power with a decisive mandate under the strong leadership of Narendra Modi, which has no major hurdle in the way to integrate the Indian economy fully into the global economy as the present government has not been crippled by the pulls and pressures of coalition politics which prevented UPA governments and previous non-Congress governments from deepening further the process of full integration with contemporary capitalism of monopolies.

Unlike the Nehruvians, the Hindu nationalist party advocates, according to its proponents, a more realistic foreign policy and security strategy. The cultural nourishment for this tradition derives from Brahmnical Hinduism, M.S. Golvalker and other Hindu Nationalist leaders. It is exclusionary and based on a selective reading of Indian History. The Hindu nationalist foreign and strategic policy believes in hardcore realism and advocates projection of India's military power beyond its borders. Instead of strategic autonomy, this school advocates alignment with the lone super power to achieve the national security goals. To Hindu nationalists, pre-emptive strikes are not anathema and defensive strategy should be replaced with offensive advancements. The Hindu Nationalists do not accept the plurality of India and they think that India is the land of Hindus. Once the primacy of Hinduism is accepted by the minorities, they will get respect for their traditions and way of life. In the backdrop of the above said political philosophy of the ruling party, we have to evaluate the foreign policy initiatives of Prime Minister Narendra Modi.

The present author would like to believe that Modi's continuous interactions with the leaders from the neighbourhood, the Japanese Prime minister, the Chinese President and, above all, with the U.S. President Barack Obama might have helped him to rediscover the merit of strategic autonomy. Immediately after inking the partnership agreement with U.S. President Obama, Prime Minister Modi asked his external affairs minister to go to China to prepare the ground for his visit to that country in May 2015.

The U.S. Defence Secretary wanted India to sign the first of the three foundational agreements—The Logistics Support Agreement (LSA) suitably tweaked for India as Logistics Exchange Memorandum of Agreement (LEMOA) during his second visit to India on April 11-12, 2016. However, in the last minute, Modi stopped the proceedings and finally Parrikar announced the acceptance of the LEMOA in principle. He added, that this agreement could be "signed in months, if not weeks". What was left unstated was that, if it meets with hostile reception and turns into a political liability, the timeline could well stretch to never. Like the impetuous announcement by Modi in Paris to buy 36 Rafale fighter aircraft and peremptorily bury the medium multi-role combat aircraft procurement process, the decision on LEMOA, initiated with much enthusiasm, too could become a bilateral issue without closure" (Karnad, 2016).

During the same period of Ashton Carter's second visit to India on April 11-12, 2016, the National Security Advisor Ajit Doval travelled to China for a strategic dialogue. The Chinese Foreign Ministry came out with a press release that Doval's discussions with State Councillor Yang Jiechi were "extensive, in-depth and candid". The operative paragraph says:

"Starting from the big picture of long-term development of bilateral relations, both sides will, with the positive attitude of mutual respect and understanding and on the basis of existing results from negotiations, stay on the track of political settlement, stick to peaceful negotiations to resolve the boundary question, meet each other half-way, and continue to promote the process of framework negotiation, so as to strive for a fair and reasonable solution that both sides accept. In the meantime, the two countries should properly manage and handle disputes, strengthen consultations on boundary affairs, and well safeguard peace and tranquillity in boundary regions, so as to create favourable conditions for the development of bilateral relations (MFA, as quoted by Bhadrakumar, 2016).

Will this politico-strategic game in the flying trapeze be long-lasting? The answer to this question is connected to the dynamics of certain constraints and imponderables. One thing is very clear. Of late the discussion is that a Modi Doctrine is in the making. This is based on an erroneous reading of his foreign policy overtures like inviting the Tibetan Prime Minister-in-exile for his swearing-in along with the SAARC leaders and his attempts to have strategic partnership with the U.S., Japan, Australia etc.

However, from a close look at what Prime Minister Modi aims to achieve, we could see strikingly similar policy objectives pursued by his immediate predecessors Manmohan Singh and A.B. Vajpayee. Neither of them constructed a doctrine of their own, but pursued a swing policy between Indira Doctrine and Gujral Doctrine, both aimed at strategic autonomy (Hall, 2015).

Prime Minister Indira Gandhi's attitude towards India's small neighbours in South Asia was more assertive and sometime hegemonic because of the regional strategic dynamics. Her neighbourhood policy has been called "hegemonic interventionism" (Hall, 2015). She entered into a treaty of peace and friendship with the Soviet Union during the peak of the East Pakistan crisis in 1971 when Bangladesh was on its birth pang. India's non-alignment was criticized as pro-Moscow. In a later period, Prime Minister Gujral wanted to remove the tag attached to India as the big brother through his doctrine of benevolence without reciprocity (Hall, 2015). He came out with the idea that India should be benevolent to the small neighbours and his neighbourhood policy came to be known as the 'Gujral Doctrine'.

In fact Indira doctrine and Gujral Doctrine are two variants of the same grand strategy rooted in the plural and democratic secular philosophy of the Congress party. As noted at the outset, the economic pronouncements of Prime Minister Modi indicated that he would continue, on a fast pace, with the reforms that was initiated in 1991 by Prime Minister Narasimha Rao and pursued by his immediate predecessors Manmohan Singh and Vajpayee.

We can observe in Narendra Modi's approach of 'strategic interconnectedness' or 'multi-vectored engagement' a striking similarity with the Nehruvian non-alignment and strategic autonomy. At the dawn of Independence, such an approach facilitated liberal capitalist economic development with socialist flavours on an upward trajectory. It shows that there existed symbiotic relationship between foreign policy strategy and domestic economic development and the nature of international political economy. It seems that Modi's 'Make in India' project would try to draw its nourishment from monopoly capitalism, and the politico-strategic doctrine will be constructed on the plank of multi-vectored alignment or strategic interconnectedness.

Strategic Autonomy or U.S.-India Strategic Handshake?

From the above, it could be gleaned that 'strategic autonomy', the quintessence of nonalignment is a fairly constant element in the foreign and strategic policy of India right from the days of Nehru, the architect of India's foreign and strategic policy. This is in fact a civilizational legacy, very well ingrained in the collective psyche of Indians. The most important aspect of strategic autonomy is that our games of autonomy are played in the lap of political economy of capitalism. Therefore, the natural course of action is that, India has to adjust and remodel its politico-strategic calculations in accordance with the shifts in the international political economy. Such an adjustment or remodelling started unfolding with the initiation of the LPG reforms in India. However, weak central governments crippled by coalition's pressures could not facilitate the expansion of dependent peripheral capitalism in India as envisaged. In the last general elections, we witnessed the collapse of the Congress system and the definitive victory for the Hindu nationalist BJP under the strong leadership of Prime Minister Narendra Modi. It was perceived that BJP's Hindu nationalism in alliance with the comprador elements in trade and commerce would pressurise Modi to further accelerate economic neo-liberalism.

The post-Cold War international power structure is symptomatic of the overarching politico-military dominance of the U.S. which turned out to be the protective shield of the international political economy managed by the Wall Street-WTO-World Bank complex. However, the U.S. initiatives to curb international terrorism and actions against state sponsored terrorism suits to New Delhi's official positions on India's strategic objectives that were reformulated in the aftermath of the collapse of the Soviet Union. In official parlance, India's relations with the United States have acquired remarkable maturity and dynamism in the post-Cold War period. Many developments created a favourable atmosphere for such a transformation, including the end of the Cold War. The U.S. perception of India's emergence as a dynamic economic force has been the driver of the above said maturity in India's relations with the U.S.

At present, the India-U.S. relations are moving beyond a bilateral partnership towards a global partnership, which is anchored not only on common values but also common interests of the dominant sections. The strategic dimension of India's relationship with the U.S. underlines their common interest in combating terrorism, proliferation of weapons of mass destruction and enhancing global peace. There has been a convergence of views on strategic and security issues which extends to cooperation in defence, science and technology, health, trade, space, energy and environment. It is worth noting that U.S. counts India on its side in the execution of the newly crafted 'rebalancing strategy in the Indo-pacific region'.

On several counts, U.S. rebalancing strategy in the Indo-

Pacific region finds strategic convergence with India's 'Look East Policy' which was drawn up in the 1990s to further cement its relations with the countries of Southeast and East Asia in the context of the disappearance of India's most trusted friend Soviet Union from the political map of the planet (Pillai, 2015). More than an external economic policy or a political slogan, the 'Look East Policy' is a strategic shift in India's vision of the world and its place in the evolving global political economy. It is also a manifestation of India's belief that developments in East Asia are of direct consequence to its security and development.

Therefore, India is actively engaged in creating a bond of friendship and cooperation with East Asia; and that has a strong economic foundation and a cooperative paradigm of positive interconnectedness of security interests. The LEP represents a reorientation of India's foreign economic policy in the aftermath of the demise of the Soviet Union and it signalled the end of the era of self-reliant growth strategy formulated by Nehru and ardently adhered to by his daughter Indira Gandhi.

Concluding Observations

It is very much astonishing to note that the foreign policy behaviour of Prime Minister Narendra Modi government with its Sangh Parivar background demonstrates a clear and striking similarity with the Nehruvian architecture of non-alignment and strategic autonomy in its new and improved version pursued by Vajpayee and Manmohan Singh. The Nehruvian framework of non-alignment did not attempt to delink from the liberal capitalist world order. Instead, the flexibility that was embedded in liberal capitalism was leveraged by the Congress of Nehru and Indira Gandhi to fulfil the objective of import substitution industrialisation—the dominant paradigm of development during that period. Since the social structure of accumulation in contemporary capitalism of monopolies is totally different from that of embedded liberalism, such leverage was hardly available for the post-reforms governments in India.

However, Narasimha Rao managed the switch over to the LPG with ease. Governments of Vajpayee and Manmohan Singh could not tune the Indian economy fully in accordance with the interests of monopoly capitalism only because of weak coalition governments and the stiff resistance offered by certain social formations in general and the left political parties in particular. Even then, both of them promoted free market economy to the extent possible.

From the above, it could be gleaned that 'strategic autonomy', the quintessence of non-alignment is a fairly constant element in the foreign policy strategy of India right from the days of Nehru, the architect of India's foreign policy. This is in fact a civilizational legacy, very well ingrained in the collective psyche of Indians. The most important aspect of strategic autonomy is that our games of autonomy are played in the lap of political economy of capitalism. Therefore, the natural course of action is that, India has to adjust and remodel its politico-strategic calculations in accordance with the shifts in the international political economy. Such an adjustment or remodelling started unfolding with the initiation of the LPG reforms in India.

However, weak central governments crippled by coalition's pressures could not facilitate the expansion of dependent peripheral capitalism in India as envisaged. In the last general elections, we witnessed the collapse of the Congress system and the definitive victory for the Hindu nationalist BJP under the strong leadership of Narendra Modi. It was perceived that BJP's Hindu nationalism in alliance with the comprador elements in trade and commerce would pressurise Modi to further accelerate economic neo-liberalism. As is the case with political Islam, it is presumed, the political project of Hindutva cultural nationalism would be at the beck and call of finance capital.

From the above understanding of the dynamics of international political economy, what emerges very clearly is that the desirable foreign policy strategy for India, a quintessential civilization, is to keep equidistance from both China and the U.S. and positive engagement with both these countries and strengthening of the BRICS initiative by all means available. Modi's capability to tread a tightrope of equidistance will be determined by the ability of the popular class, or rather the *Aam Aadmi,* in checkmating the adventurism of the comprador class to subordinate the Indian economy unconditionally to the international political economy controlled by finance capital.

References

Amin, S. (2006), "Beyond U.S. Hegemony"?, Zed Books: London.

Bhadrakumar, M.K. (2016), "The Geopolitics of Ash Carter's India Visit". *Punchline,* May 15, 2016.

—(2016), "Modi Government is Acting like a Bull in China Shop", *Punchline*, April 21, 2016.

Brezinski, Zbigniew (2016), "Towards a Global Realignment", *The American Interest*, April 17, 2016.

Hall, I. (2015), "Is a Modi Doctrine Emerging in Indian Foreign Policy", *Australian Journal of International Affairs.*

Hagerty, D.T. (2009), "India and the Global Balance of Power: A Neo-realist Snapshot", in Harsh V. Pant (ed.), 'Indian Foreign Policy in a Unipolar World'.

Harvey D. (2007), "A Brief History of Neo-liberalism", Oxford.

Jaffrelot, C. (2014), "A Modi Doctrine"?, *Indian Express* November 20.

Karnad, B. (2014), "America an Unreliable Partner", *The New Indian Express,* January 24.

—(2014), "Home Grown Islamic Terrorism", *The New Indian Express,* October 24.

—(2016), "India's Foreign Policy: The Foreign Hand", *Open Magazine,* March 29.

—(2016), "Has PM Modi Developed Cold Feet over Logistic Agreement with the US"?, *The Citizen,* April 14.

—(2016), "India in America's Coils"? *The Citizen*, March 11.

Karat, P. (2016), "Bharat Mata with Stars and Stripes", *The Citizen,* April 8.

Raju, R. (2013), "India's Security: Emerging Frontiers of

Cooperation", in Mohanan B. Pillai (ed.), 'India's National Security: Concerns and Strategies', New Delhi: New Century Publications.

Pant, Harsh V. (ed.) (2009), "Indian Foreign Policy in a Unipolar World", New Delhi: Routledge.

Pillai, M.B. (2015), "U.S. Rebalancing Strategy in the Indo-Pacific Region", in Josukutty, C.A. (ed.), 'India-U.S. Relations and Asian Rebalancing', New Delhi: New Century Publications.

—-(2015), "India's Strategic Thinking and Policy Options', in Suresh R. (ed.), 'The Changing Dimensions of Security: India's Security Policy Options', New Delhi: Vij.

Saran, S (2014), "BRICS: The End of Western Dominance of the Global Financial and Economic Order", *Interpress Service,* July 23.

Srinivasan, K. (2013), "India's Security Policy: Shifting Paradigms and Emerging Frontiers", in Mohanan B. Pillai (ed.), 'India's National Security: Concerns and Strategies', New Delhi: New Century Publications.

4

Maritime Security and Contemporary India

S. Utham Kumar Jamadhagni

Blue State

India in the contemporary world is looking to continue its modest growth in the economic sector while also attempting to increase its presence in the world political schema. While the Asian Century is providing her with the opportunity to possibly steer world economic affairs in the near future, there are several challenges facing her in many other fields.

The tests of her ability to cope with growing problems stems both from internal demands of a burgeoning middle class with added purchasing power as well as a widening poverty populace that needs additional focus and impetus. She must also cater to external issues of precarious regional security architecture that continuously lays strain on her defence capabilities. The efforts to counter terrorism threats and be in step with growing Chinese footprint in our area of influence bring to the fore, questions about her preparedness and efficiency.

This article specifically looks at maritime security aspect in India's contemporary period. As a maritime nation, much of India's contact with the outside world flourished through the maritime routes. It not only brought Indian products to far off lands but also forged cultural influences that are carried to this day. Despite her primary position in the Indian Ocean, her modern outlook on geo-strategy has not accorded appropriate status to its maritime aspect. It is only in the wake of the 26/11 attacks that there has been an emphasis on maritime vulnerability and consequent need for preparedness. The vast coastline often means open borders where every inch is vulnerable to incursion. The non-traditional threats to maritime security have increased with various acts of piracy, maritime terrorism, human and narcotic trafficking and illegal fishing in the immediate oceanic neighbourhood. Understanding the challenges is only one side of the coin. Addressing these challenges needs prowess.

First, let us discuss the existing capabilities in this respect. The Indian Navy, the main arm defending the vast coastline, is relatively small in comparison to its service counterparts, the Army and the Air Force. Often termed the "Cinderella Service", [1] Navy garners only 16 percent of India's defence budgetary outlay. [2] This modest allocation now has to cater to a massive modernisation drive that seeks to revamp an ageing fleet in tune with current and future problems that affect maritime security at large.

Present Status

To establish and maintain its sway in its immediate maritime neighbourhood, India requires an effective and modern marine fleet. With her sights set on transforming into a "Blue Water Navy", there is need to keenly examine her physical assets. The actual Indian Naval fleet comprises of warships, cruisers, submarines, fast attack crafts etc. However, much of her fleet is ageing.

One aircraft carrier has been decommissioned while only two others *INS Viraat* and *INS Vikramaditya* are in service. *INS Vikramaditya* has been purchased from Russia and has seen huge cost over runs and delays. Recently, India unveiled plans for a second indigenous aircraft carrier. [3] Others like submarines, await refit. For example, only half of her 13 diesel-electric submarines are operational at any one time due to refit schedules. *INS Sindhughosh* met with an accident when a fishing boat damaged its periscope in 2015. [4] A couple of years earlier another submarine *INS Sindhurakshak* sunk after blasts in the torpedo section. [5] The string of accidents in recent years has also not helped the fleet strength. [6]

Corvettes, warships and submarines have also been involved in accidents in recent years. [7] The fall out was the resignation of Chief of Naval Staff, Admiral D.K. Joshi. [8] The ageing fleet is being cited as one of the reasons for the frequency of accidents.

With indigenous attempts at manufacture hit by delays, the only option was import and that too second-hand ones due to prohibitive capital expenditure in purchase of new ones. [9] Though India has the third largest armed forces in the world, her defence procurement leaves much to be desired. Nearly a third of the budget outlay goes to capital acquisitions. The time lag between the drawing board and actual operational physical assets has accentuated the reliability on imports to satisfy short-term demands. In fact, 60 percent of India's defence needs are catered to by imports only. According to the latest SIPRI report, India continues to be the world's largest importer of arms which has been so for nearly a decade now. [10] The dependency is nearly 70 percent and it has been found that public sector alone cannot achieve self-reliance. [11] Producing under license also means neither indigenisation as well as lack of innovation.

In a CAG report tabled in 2008 to the Indian Parliament, it was said, "'With serious slippages in the induction plan, Navy is left with an ageing fleet with more than 50 percent of its submarines having completed 75 percent of their operational life. Some have already outlived their maximum service life", [12] while others have seen the light of day only after inordinate delays and cost over-runs. [13] There are also questions of optimising efficiency that can be achieved only with external support. For example, in the case of the inshore patrol vessel for the Coast Guard *Rani Durgavati*, though indigenously built, the large size of the craft meant lower speed. [14] The Australian Company, Thorncroft Maritime, helped to improve efficiency by fitting it with three water jet propulsion systems. [15] The old mine sweepers that were in service were only the modified versions of Soviet *Natya* class subs.

DPP Change

In a concerted effort to alter the external dependence of defence equipment supply, the current government has proposed drastic changes in the defence procurement policy. It seeks to revise the procedure every year to respond appropriately to contemporary changes. Emphasis has been placed on purchasing and building in India as compared to buying off the shelves from the global market. The new category of Indian designed, developed and manufactured products catapult incentives to 'higher-tech realm of designing and developing Indian weaponry'. [16] Earlier, the emphasis was on domestic manufacturing of foreign-origin equipment. It was also vague on the vital points like intellectual property rights (IPRs), R&D and innovations. [17]

Streamlining of indigenous production by relaxing the private investment cap; deregulation of dual use items under the Industrial Licenses Act of 1951 and encouragement of FDI up to 100 percent in certain areas are some of the key proposals under the refurbished purchase policy. Foreign companies must mandatorily procure 30 percent of the supplies from Indian partners in case of a bid being ₹ 2,000 crore or more. [18] This clause would provide fillip to domestic manufacturing. Joint ventures have also received impetus—the allowance of 15 percent for machinery worth more than ₹ 1 billion installed and similar additional deduction for over ₹ 250 million worth new plants and machinery. The expectation is to shift India's standing as a prime importer to 'being a producer of trail-blazing technology'. [19]

Make in India and Navy

Prime Minister Narendra Modi, in his maiden Independence address unveiled the "Make in India" initiative that aims to bring global manufacturing to India. One of the key sectors to benefit from this program is the defence sector. The know-how of the global defence manufacturing industry will be tied in with Indian public and private sector companies to set up and augment India's defence manufacturing capabilities. In response to the 'Make in India' initiative, the defence companies both foreign and Indian, big and small have joined to form the Association for Defence Companies (ADC) to provide a unified voice on policy matters and promote interests of all defence related businesses. [20]

For the Indian Navy that is in dire need of modernisation, this could be a shot in the arm. India has now embarked on one of the most ambitious warship-building programmes in the world. [21] The target of 200-ship navy to be achieved in the coming decade will augment the current fleet of 14 submarines, 27 combatants, 100 coastal combatants and two squadrons of patrol aircraft.

Indigenously made naval equipment including frigates, helicopters, submarines are now either being delivered or have commenced production. The anti-submarine warfare corvettes *INS Kamorta* and *INS Kadmatt* have been built indigenously by Garden Reach Shipbuilders and Engineers, Kolkata and handed to the Navy recently. [22] According to Admiral R.K. Dhowan, private sector would now be building warships too, as illustrated by orders for naval offshore patrol vessels, cadet training ships and floating docks. [23]

Global operators are now free to choose appropriate private players for joint ventures. An example would be Russia choosing the Pipavav shipyard of Reliance Group to manufacture *Talwar* class frigates. Refit of submarines are also being carried with foreign assistance in Indian shipyards.

The first of the French Scorpene diesel-electric attack submarines, *INS Kalvari* will be commissioned later this year from the Mazagon docks. Six more are in the pipeline. [24, 25] Under a recent agreement, a French ship building company GTT, has offered LNG ship building technology to India's Cochin Shipyard. This would enable it to compete for a GAIL contract for LNG ships that could each cost US$ 200-300 million. [26] The shipyard has now received certification to build LNG ships making India the fourth country to join the elite group of South Korea, Japan and China in this specialisation. [27]

Three Kolkata class guided missile destroyers *INS Kolkata, INS Kochi* and the yet to be inducted *INS Chennai* are indigenously built with domestic made sensors and other systems. [28] Yet another feather in the cap is the *INS Astradharini*, the torpedo launch and recovery vessel fruit of joint collaboration between the NSTL Naval Science and Technological Laboratory of the DRDO, a private operator Shoft Shipyard of Bharuch, Gujarat and IIT, Kharagpur. [29] It has made an important contribution in indigenous weapons development.

Capacity building has also picked up pace with a MoU signed between Reliance and Andhra Pradesh government for the biggest investment for a ship building project of ₹ 5,000 crore at Rambilli near Vishakapatnam. [30]

The Central Government has accorded infrastructure status to ship building in January 2016. [31] This would facilitate funding and long-term loans for a strategically important industry. It has a high multiplier effect on investment, turnover and high employment potential. [32] Last year, the government earmarked ₹ 10,000 crore as ship building development fund to enable fleet operators to buy Indian built ships. [33] The 2016 budget exempts excise duty on capital goods and related spares for ship repairs undertaken by ship building companies in India. [34] The "Make in India" initiative would receive boost if start-up companies that are developing high-end defence application devices or technologies are offered finance for research efforts. [35]

Looking Beyond

The next point of focus is expanding India's maritime area of interest. The recently released Navy publication titled 'Ensuring Secure Seas: Indian Maritime Security Strategy', lists out the *primary and secondary areas of maritime* interest. In the recent documents, the area of primary interest has expanded from northern Indian Ocean region to southwest Indian Ocean and Red Sea. Secondary area includes West Africa and the Mediterranean Sea. Though these centre around the Indian Ocean, the mention of "other areas of national interest based on considerations of...overseas investments...", [36] could mean focus on regions like South America where India now has gas and petroleum investments. India also sees itself as a "net maritime security provider". [37] A further expansion to include East African coast and South America would be advisable.

Latin America is gaining focus. India has increased its diplomatic missions from 7 to 14. India has also increased her interaction with this far away continent. Peru has joined Brazil, Venezuela, Mexico, Chile, Colombia, and Argentina as countries that have more than a billion US dollars in trade with India. [38] India has signed a PTA with Chile. India has made Bolivia's largest FDI of US$ 2.3 billion in an iron ore mine. When China stopped buying Argentinean Soybean oil in 2010, India stepped in and helped by tripling its import of this commodity from the South American state. Peru's principal export to India is copper while India exports iron and steel products. IT sector can be another area where India can augment its investment. [39]

Fuel Folio

Energy security is yet another aspect where new regions like Latin America need to be looked at. India has concentrated its relations with Brazil alone. It now needs to diversify. India has become the 3rd largest oil importer in the world after U.S. and China. After the West Asian region, South America has emerged as the second largest provider of oil for India with 19 percent of total import volume [40] nudging Africa to third position. India has also invested nearly US$ 3 billion in Venezuela, Brazil and Columbia in oil fields. The increase in procurement from the Latino region is not only cost effective but also makes business sense as it augments Indian refining capacities as a profit making venture catering to the external demands. [41] It is cost effective and hence maritime relations must be improved. India has a healthy trade relation with these countries that must be used as a launching pad to extend into areas like naval relations.

Common Cause

Interestingly, all South American countries have vast coastlines and maritime security could be another area of common interest for India. [42] Brazil's naval modernisation plans to safeguard its newly found off-shore oil assets could be a prospective area of cooperation for India. [43] Brazil's naval acquisitions run parallel to Indian efforts including acquisition of an aircraft carrier; scorpene class submarines, as well as nuclear powered ones. [44] Chile is also embarking on strengthening its navy. It seeks to enhance its sea denial capabilities. It has acquired frigates, scorpene submarines from France and off-shore patrol vessels from Germany. [45] Argentina is also looking to foreign powers to provide naval modernisation help. [46]

While most of her earlier ships and submarines were of German origin, now Argentina is gaining French assistance to acquire amphibious assault ships. The government also has a Research and Development Progressive Program similar to India's "Make in India" plan to modernise and restore the shipping system. Under this scheme, four corvettes and two submarines are set to be revamped. [47] The drive towards indigenous development could be a common platform for both countries to interact. Also, many of the South American countries face drug trafficking menace through the maritime routes. [48] According to Ana Lilia Perez, author of *Mares de Cocaina* (Seas of Cocaine), 70 to 80 percent of cocaine consumed worldwide is trafficked at some point via sea. [49] Anti-smuggling operations can be another cooperative launch pad between Indian Navy and her South American counterparts.

Spread of the Red

Not only must India counter increased influence of China in our immediate neighbourhood but also in hitherto neglected regions like Latin America. In keeping with its worldwide expansion of interest and influence, China has stepped up its interaction with South American countries. China is now South America's second largest export destination. [50] China is also the largest creditor for Ecuador, Venezuela and Argentina. China has been made satellites for Venezuela and Bolivia. [51] In fact, in the case of Bolivia, the satellite was not only mostly funded by China but it earned valuable exchange for the Bolivians. [52] China is making headway into these countries too, by offering high technological help like satellite launches. To enable smoother transport of resources from these countries to China, a trans-Andean railway is proposed to be built at a cost of US$ 10 billion. [53] India also has other advantages like sizable English speaking population, a market for Latin American goods and a more independent business climate which could be utilised. [54]

Benign Action

Humanitarian and disaster relief operations recently undertaken by Indian Navy shows that the benign role of this arm of the services could come in handy more frequently. There has been increased frequency of climate change related natural calamities and problems due to civil strife. *Operation Raahat* rescued 4,000 Indians and nearly a 1,000 foreigners belonging to 26 countries including United States from Yemen. [55] *INS Sumitra, INS Mumbai, INS Tarkash* and *MV Kavaratti and Corals* were involved in the relief work. [56] The last two are domestic ships that brought back 1,200 Indians stranded in the war torn country. [57] Even in the recent Chennai floods, the *INS Airavat*—the amphibious warship, *INS Shakti, INS Shayadri* were pressed into service. [58] The Navy rescued stranded persons and distributed food packets. This was the largest rescue operation since the 2004 tsunami. [59] More and more such efforts could occur in the near future.

Prospects

One other area could be the Coast Guard complementing the Indian Navy in many of the areas mentioned above. Indian Coast Guard recently conducted a joint exercise with its Japanese counterpart with its ship ECHIGO off Chennai in January 2016. [60] It had also sent its ship *Sankalp,* an advanced offshore patrol vessel to Darwin, Australia in 2014 on the heels of signing a joint Framework for security cooperation by Indian Prime Minister Narendra Modi and his Australian counterpart Tony Abbott to further maritime cooperation. [61]

The Coast Guard has worked in tandem with the Indian Navy and other agencies in patrolling the coasts to detect potential threats and mitigate them in good time. [62] In 2012, the Coast Guard caught 135 Bangladeshis off an island in the Andamans. [63] Last month, they intercepted a Pakistani boat illegally entering the Kutch coast and arrested 11 fishermen. [64] Not only is the coastal security a priority for this sea-based force but even marine pollution. The Director General Coast Guard has been made responsible for National Oil Spill Disaster Contingency Plans (NOSDCP) and coordinates in all efforts to prevent marine pollution from ships, ports and facilities in India. [65] It also provides training to the shipping and oil industry. Sensitive duties like the manning of the International Maritime Boundary Line (IMBL) in the Palk Bay and checking poaching of endangered marine species are also carried out by the Indian Coast Guard. [66] Narcotics have also been captured in this region. [67]

Other areas of maritime security like ocean governance must also be looked into. Resource utilisation and environmental conservation together with sustainable development must become part of India's ocean governance agenda. The over exploitation of marine resources is of concern to India. Management of resources and scientific solutions to augment resource utilisation can be areas of renewed interest. Though an Ocean Policy was announced as early as 1982, [68] not much has been done from the policy angle since. The statement deals almost entirely with the economic and industrial wealth of the oceans and the need to utilize utmost human potential to tap this. [69]

Phenomenal work has gone into the setting up of a national research and development infrastructure complete with a separate government department of ocean development and a host of other institutions that focus on the scientific, geographic, marine and economic features of the Indian Ocean. The National Institutes for Oceanography, Ocean Technology, Port Management and Ocean Management and research centres in institutes of excellence like IIT and Anna University are examples of this effort. However, integration at the policy level is not reflected even in the 'Vision 2015' document.

The management, control and authority over the resource rich ocean waters are handled by as many as 12 ministries and 17 departments. However, a separate department has been set up to manage the oceanic scientific and technological activity, namely the Department of Ocean Development. The concept of integrated coastal management has also gained ground in India and several legislative and policy initiatives have indicated the ocean awareness of the government. Limited capacity of various agencies for law enforcement and the need for amendment of such laws and policies are some pertinent issues. The loss of coastal marine bio-diversity is due to a variety of factors like poor management of the resources; lack of proper understanding of complex coastal and marine ecosystem which results in injudicious exploitation of natural resources; lack of people's involvement; lack of proper legislation and policies, and multiplicity of management agencies.

Post-9/11 maritime security also came under renewed focus. The International Maritime Organisation (IMO) Assembly called for a thorough review of all existing measures to combat acts of violence and crime at sea. The most far-reaching security measure is the International Ship and Port Facility Security Code—the ISPS Code. [70] This provides a consistent, standardized framework for evaluating risk and counter threats with changes in vulnerability for ships and port facilities through the determination of appropriate security levels and corresponding security measures. [71]

In all, India's natural outlet is towards the sea, through which 95 percent of its overseas trade passes. The country's sea lanes are economically important and serve as vital seaborne trade routes through the Indian Ocean. Thus, safety of sea lanes is of prime maritime interest. India's other maritime interests include high value assets in the form of offshore oil and the vast potential of minerals and seabed resources in the waters surrounding it. As an energy dependent economy and an oil dependent country, India's maritime links are of prime importance. India's rising economy and commensurate phenomenal increase for oil and concomitantly her sea dependence is only bound to increase. In addition, India has fishing interests in its EEZ, safe guarding vital fishing grounds and the abundant fish stock in the Indian Ocean. The local ship building industry is expected to witness resurgence due to the 'Make in India' plan. The growth of the Indian Navy has mainly been commensurate with the country's expanding maritime interests, and should be viewed in that context.

The confusion and debate surrounding even programs of national importance like the Sethu Samudram Ship Canal Project indicate the distance that is needed to be travelled. Slack in preparedness or capacity building to implement 'Agenda 21, Chapter 17', that looks at ocean governance from a holistic perspective, [72] is seen as a principal lacuna in factoring ocean governance into India's maritime security rubric. With an ever increasing reliance on the ocean for economic, strategic and environmental purposes, it is time for India to chart a fresh, combined and all inclusive course, which could only include integrated ocean's management as a beginning.

Conclusion

The changing global environment with emphasis on economic progress has shifted the pivot towards Asia. With an appreciable growth due to a liberalised economy, a fast expanding middle class with an increased purchasing power and a clear shift of manufacture and sale of goods from the West towards her, India at the present and in the near future will continue to garner heightened attention. However, this higher status accrues challenges too.

In the field of maritime security which is vital to India's

burgeoning trade ties with countries beyond the immediate realm, present day India faces opportunities and threats. Piracy, maritime terrorism, smuggling, illegal fishing and over exploitation of marine resources are some non-traditional threats that can affect Indian security in the maritime dimension. An examination of naval preparedness brings out several concerns. The physical capacity of the Indian Navy has been hampered by the lack of state-of-the-art technology in ships and slack in indigenous design and development of all aspects of a sea worthy navy.

Some of these defects are being addressed by policy changes more significantly, like the "Make in India" plan that seeks to boost local manufacturing and more importantly develop ships and all related equipment. The idea has borne fruit to a certain extent. However, there is a long way to go. The importance of foreign assistance to assuage short term requirements has also been factored into.

Moving to areas that have hitherto not received adequate attention like Latin America and its potential contribution to energy security, naval modernisation could be attempted. It must also be borne in mind that China has been progressing rapidly in gaining influence in this region through trade and financial means. India must continue her contribution in offering relief during periods of calamity and disaster.

Appreciating the contribution of the Indian Coast Guard in maintaining maritime security and deepening its involvement can also be undertaken. Finally, concepts like ocean governance can be accorded more impetus and make maritime security truly comprehensive in scope and reach.

Strategically, the Indian Ocean has remained the mainstay of Indian naval ambitions. In fact, the publication of India's Maritime Doctrine is quite explicit on the central status of the Indian Ocean in India's strategic thought and on India's determination to constitute the most important influence in the region as a whole. Maritime power for national prosperity being the goal means all areas that have commercial and energy interests as well as new areas that are emerging should be in focus. Though there are several issues in maritime security that could help contemporary India achieve its immediate goals, how we are able to sustain, build and improve upon its requirements will shape our maritime future. In the contemporary world, India must utilise the opportunities for change and counter challenges to maritime security by broadening its scope, deepening its engagement and enhancing its capacity in every field of maritime activity.

Endnotes

1. As quoted in James Holmes, Andrew Winner and Toshi Yoshihara (2009), "Indian Naval Strategy in the Twenty-first Century", Routledge.
2. Laxman Behera, "India's Defence Budget 2015-16", *Issue Brief,* IDSA March 2, 2015, available at: http://www.idsa.in/issuebrief/IndiasDefenceBudget2015-16_lkbehera_020315.
3. http://nationalinterest.org/blog/the-buzz/india-building-second-homegrown-aircraft-carrier-13375.
4. "Navy Submarine INS Sindhughosh Collides with Fishing Boat, Suffers Periscope Damage, *The Times of India*, February 22, 2015, available at: http://timesofindia.indiatimes.com/india/Navy-submarine-INS-Sindhughosh-collides-with-fishing-boat-suffers-periscope-damage/articleshow/46335295.cms.
5. "Midnight Blasts Sink INS Sindhurakshak", *The Hindu*, August 15, 2013, available at: http://www.thehindu.com/news/national/midnight-blasts-sink-ins-sindhurakshak/article5020065.ece.
6. http://www.ibtimes.co.in/india-modernise-its-aging-naval-fleet-china-increases-presence-indian-ocean-616002.
7. For a list of some of these accidents see, http://www.dnaindia.com/india/report-indian-navy-11-accidents-22-deaths-in-seven-months-1967635.
8. "Indian Navy Chief Quits After Submarine Accident", *Reuters*, February 26, 2014, available at: http://www.reuters.com/article/us-india-submarine-resign-idUSBREA1P11T20140226.

9. http://www.defencenow.com/news/145/indian-navy-to-get-south-korean-minesweepers-in-its-fleet.html.
10. "India Retains World's Largest Weapons Importer Tag", *The Hindu*, February 23, 2016, available at: http://www.thehindu.com/news/national/india-retains-worlds-largest-weapons-importer-tag/article8271899.ece.
11. "Defence Production and Import Dependency in India", *General Knowledge Today*, January 2, 2016, available at: http://www.gktoday.in/blog/defence-production-and-import-dependency-in-india.
12. "Defending India: An Ageing Naval Fleet, Obsolete Equipment", *The Times of India*, October 25, 2008, available at: http://timesofindia.indiatimes.com/india/Defending-India-An-ageing-naval-fleet-obsolete-equipment/articleshow/3638790.cms.
13. "Two Indian Coast Guard Ships Commissioned at Naval Dock", *The Times of India*, September 21, 2015, available at: http://timesofindia.indiatimes.com/city/mumbai/Two-Indian-Coast-Guard-ships-commissioned-at-Naval-Dock/articleshow/49047985.cms.
14. http://www.thornycroftmaritime.com.au/viewStory/Company+Achievements.
15. "Patrol Vessel Sails from Hindustan Shipyard", *Deccan Chronicle*, June 6, 2015, available at: http://www.deccanchronicle.com/150606/nation-current-affairs/article/patrol-vessel-sails-hindustan-shipyard-ltd.
16. "Parrikar's Proposed Defence Procurement Policy Breaks New Ground", *Business Standard*, January 13, 2016, available at: http://www.business-standard.com/article/economy-policy/parrikar-s-proposed-defence-procurement-policy-breaks-new-ground-116011300037_1.html.
17. Sandeep Varma, "India's Defence Procurement Procedure: Assessing the Case for Review and Reforms", *Issue Brief*, IDSA, available at: http://www.idsa.in/issuebrief/IndiasDefenceProcurementProcedure_sverma_171014.
18. "New Defence Procurement Procedure Changes Dynamics", *The Tribune*, January 11, 2016, available at: http://www.tribuneindia.com/news/nation/new-defence-procurement-procedure-changes-dynamics/182217.html.
19. "New Defence Procurement Policy Promises to Make Defence

Market More Lucrative", *The Indian Express*, January 12, 2016, available at:
http://indianexpress.com/article/explained/new-defence-procurement-policy-promises-to-make-defense-market-more-lucrative.

20. "Make in India Push: Defence Companies to Form Industry Alliance", *The Economic Times*, October 6, 2015.
21. http://thewire.in/2015/12/03/between-china-terror-and-the-deep-blue-sea-indias-new-naval-doctrine-takes-shape-16665.
22. "Indian Navy Gets Second Indigenous Antisubmarine Warship 'Kadmatt', *The Economic Times*, November 26, 2015, available at: http://economictimes.indiatimes.com/news/defence/indiannavygetssecondindigenousantisubmarinewarshipkadmatt.
23. "Private Sector Getting into Warship Building Projects: Navy Chief Admiral R.K. Dhowan", *The Economic Times*, February 3, 2016, available at:
http://economictimes.indiatimes.com/news/defence/private-sector-getting-into-warship-building-projects-navy-chief-admiral-rk-dhowan/articleshow/50827744.cms.
24. "INS Kalvari Sea Trials Begin Today: All You Need to Know About the Attack Submarine", *The Indian Express,* December 25, 2015, available at:
http://indianexpress.com/article/explained/ins-kalvari-sea-trials-begin-today-all-you-need-to-know-about-the-attack-submarine.
25. "Kalvari Submarine Set Afloat", *The Economic Times*, November 2, 2015, available at:
http://economictimes.indiatimes.com/slideshows/infrastructure/indigenously-built-scorpene-class-kalvari-submarine-set-afloat/kalvari-submarine-set-afloat/slideshow/49625446.cms.
26. "GTT to Offer India LNG Shipbuilding Tech", *The Financial Express*, December 22, 2015, available at:
http://www.financialexpress.com/article/economy/gtt-to-offer-india-lng-shipbuilding-tech/182400.
27. "India Joins Select Club to Build LNG Ships", *The Hindu*, December 21, 2015, available at:
http://www.thehindu.com/business/Industry/indiajoinsselectclubtobuildlngships/article8014684.ece.
28. "INS Kochi Set to Join the Fleet", *The Hindu*, September 28, 2015, available at:
http://www.thehindu.com/news/cities/mumbai/ins-kochi-set-to-

join-the-fleet/article7698986.ece.
29. "INS Astradharini Joins the Indian Navy", *Press release*, October 2015, available at: http://indiannavy.nic.in/content/ins-astradharini-joins-indian-navy.
30. "Anil Ambani Led Reliance Group Announces ₹ 5,000 Crore Naval Facility Investment", *The Economic Times*, January 10, 2016, available at: http://economictimes.indiatimes.com/news/defence/anil-ambani-led-reliance-group-announces-rs-5000-crore-naval-facility-investment/articleshow/50520223.cms.
31. "Infrastructure Status Granted to Shipyard Industry", *The Economic Times*, Jan 20, 2016, available at: http://articles.economictimes.indiatimes.com/2016-01-20/news/69931120_1_infrastructure-status-Indian-shipyards-shipbuilding-industry.
32. "Government to Encourage Indian Shipbuilding and Repair Industry Under Make in India", *The Business Standard*, December 9, 2015, available at: http://www.business-standard.com/article/news-cm/govt-to-encourage-indian-shipbuilding-and-repair-industry-under-make-in-india-115120901305_1.html.
33. "Government to Encourage ₹ 10,000 Crore Shipbuilding Fund", *Livemint e-paper*, February 28, 2015, available at: http://www.livemint.com/Home-age/FLnnkcHLthYMuAzLTEBaAN/Govt-considering-Rs10000-crore-shipbuilding-fund-in-budget.html.
34. "Budget 2016: Government Proposes 14 percent Service Tax on Shipping Companies Importing Goods", *The Business Standard*, February 29, 2016, available at: http://www.business-standard.com/budget/article/budget-2016-govt-proposes-14-service-tax-on-shipping-companies-importing-goods-116022900713_1.html.
35. "Hi-tech Start-ups Urge PM's Support to Ignite Defence Industry", *The Hindu*, January 11, 2016, available at: http://www.thehindu.com/business/Industry/hitech-startups-urge-pms-support-to-ignite-defence-industry/article8089347.ece.
36. "Ensuring Secure Seas: Indian Maritime Security Strategy", Integrated Headquarters, Ministry of Defence, 2015, pp. 31-32.
37. Ibid., p. 80.
38. "Peru: India's New Billion-dollar Trade Partner in Latin

America", September 12, 2013, available at: http://www.gatewayhouse.in/peru-indias-new-billion-dollar-trade-partner-in-latin-america.

39. "India-Peru: A New Pacific Pivot", *Americas Quarterly*, August 20, 2012, available at: http://www.americasquarterly.org/india-peru-a-new-pacific-pivot.
40. http://www.businesswithlatinamerica.com/business.html.
41. "Oil Imports Get a Distinct Latino Flavour", *The Financial Express*, December 9, 2015, available at: http://www.financialexpress.com/article/industry/companies/oil-imports-get-a-distinct-latino-flavour/176296.
42. http://piracy-studies.org/rising-powers-in-maritime-security-comparing-the-strategies-of-brazil-and-india.
43. "Aditya Malhotra, Brazil's Oil Future: The New (Big) Kid on the Block", *Journal of Energy Security*, April 19, 2012, available at: http://ensec.org/index.php?option=com_content&view=article&id=346:brazils-bright-oil-future&catid=123:content&Itemid=389.
44. "Rethinking Defence: Naval Modernisation", October 28, 2013, available at: http://www.naval-technology.com/features/feature-rethinking-defence-naval-modernisation-south-america.
45. Grant Turnbull, "Rethinking Defence: Naval Modernisation in South America", October 28, 2013, available at: http://www.naval-technology.com/features/feature-rethinking-defence-naval-modernisation-south-america.
46. "Armada Argentina", January 20, 2015, available at: http://www.globalsecurity.org/military/world/argentina/navy-modernization.htm.
47. Ibid.
48. Lichtenwald, Terrance G., Mara H. Steinhour, and Frank S. Perri, "A Maritime Threat Assessment of Sea Based Criminal Organizations and Terrorist Operations", *Homeland Security Affairs,* 8, Article 13, August 2012, available at: https://www.hsaj.org/articles/227.
49. http://www.insightcrime.org/news-analysis/maritime-drug-trafficking.
50. "China and Latin America: What You Need to Know", *Council on Hemispheric Affairs*, July 29, 2015, available at: http://www.coha.org/china-and-latin-america-what-you-need-to-know.

51. "China Launches Earth-observing Satellite for Venezuela", October 1, 2012, available at: http://www.space.com/17849-china-satellite-launch-venezuela.html.
52. "Chinese-Made Satellite Earns $16 Million for Bolivia", June 25, 2015, available at: http://en.yibada.com/articles/40924/20150625/chinese-made-satellite-16-million-bolivia.htm.
53. "South America News: Peru, Brazil, China Roll Ahead With Transcontinental Railway", *Latin Times*, May 14, 2015, available at: http://www.latintimes.com/south-america-news-peru-brazil-china-roll-ahead-transcontinental-railway-316465.
54. Andres Oppenheimer, "Move Over, China: Latin America May Welcome India", June 20, 2015, available at: http://www.miamiherald.com/news/local/news-columns-blogs/andres-oppenheimer/article24993673.html.
55. "Why Operation Rahat is a Major Achievement for India", *The Huffington Post*, April 8, 2015, available at: http://www.huffingtonpost.in/kabir-taneja/why-operation-rahat-is-a-_b_7023266.html.
56. http://www.ndtv.com/india-news/government-expected-to-wrap-up-yemen-evacuation-operation-today-4000-indians-rescued-so-far-753135.
57. "Two Ships Leave Kochi to Djibouti Port to Evacuate Indians in Yemen", *Zee News*, March 30, 2015, available at: http://zeenews.india.com/news/india/two-ships-leaves-kochi-to-djibouti-port-to-evacuate-indians-in-yemen_1570084.html.
58. "Navy Rushes Amphibious Ship to Chennai for Relief Ops", *The Hindu*, December 3, 2015, available at: http://www.thehindu.com/news/national/navy-rushes-amphibious-ship-to-chennai-for-relief-ops/article7942001.ece.
59. "Chennai Floods: Navy Throws a Lifeline; Brings 3 Ships and 300 Tonnes of Food", *The Deccan Chronicle*, December 5, 2015, available at: http://www.deccanchronicle.com/151205/nation-current-affairs/article/chennai-flood-navy-throws-lifeline.
60. "Indo-Japan Coast Guard Joint Exercise Conducted in the Bay of Bengal", *The Indian Express*, January 15, 2016, available at: http://newspot.me/n/01dgIVJF?original=true.
61. "Indian Coast Guard Ship in Australia to Boost Maritime Security

Ties", *Outlook*, December 4, 2014, available at: http://www.outlookindia.com/newswire/story/indian-coast-guard-ship-in-australia-to-boost-maritime-security-ties/870949.

62. "Maharashtra Coastal Security Exercise: News and Updates", available at: http://www.indiannavy.nic.in/content/maharashtra-coastal-security-exercise.
63. "Indian Coast Guard Nabs 135 Bangladeshis in Andamans", *The Economic Times*, April 3, 2012, available at: http://articles.economictimes.indiatimes.com/2012-04-03/news/31281251_1_bangladeshi-nationals-indian-coast-guard-icg.
64. "Indian Coast Guard Intercepts Pakistan Fishing Boat in Kutch: 11 Held", *The Economic Times*, February 6, 2016, available at: http://economictimes.indiatimes.com/news/ defence/indian-coast-guard-intercepts-pakistan-fishing-boat-in-kutch-11-held/articleshow/50877467.cms.
65. "Kudos to the Indian Coast Guard on its 40th Raising Day", *South Asia Analysis*, Paper No. 6068, February 2, 2016, available at: http://www.southasiaanalysis.org/node/1939.
66. "Coast Guard Captures Boat Carrying Banned Marine Species off Tamil Nadu Coast", *The Times of India*, June 14, 2015, available at: http://timesofindia.indiatimes.com/city/chennai/Coast-Guard-captures-boat-carrying-banned-marine-species-off-Tamil-Nadu-coast/articleshow/47663470.cms.
67. "Biggest Haul of Ganja in Palk Bay", *Deccan Chronicle*, June 17, 2015, available at: http://www.deccanchronicle.com/150617/nation-crime/article/biggest-haul-ganja-palk-bay.
68. "Pursuit and Promotion of Science", available at: http://www.iisc.ernet.in/insa/ch35.pdf.
69. For full text of the statement see, http://moes.gov.in/writereaddata /files/ocean%20policy%20statement(3).pdf.
70. For a complete understanding of ISPS code, refer to IMO website, http://www.imo.org/blast/mainframe.asp?topic_id=897.
71. https://www.gov.uk/guidance/maritime-security.
72. For complete text of chapter 17, refer to UN website, http://www.un.org/depts/los/consultative_process/documents/A21-Ch17.htm.

5

Maritime Threats from South of India

Jacob Ashik Bonofer

"Whoever attains maritime supremacy in the Indian Ocean would be a prominent player on the international scene"

—US Navy geo-strategist Rear Admiral Alfred Thayus Mahan (1840-1914).

Mahan was such a visionary who understood, that Indian Ocean was a pivot in the international arena and the one who controls it will be a power to be reckoned with. No wonder the historical accounts demonstrated that the Europeans, Americans and Chinese have always attempted to gain supremacy over the Indian Ocean. Talking about the significance of the Indian Ocean, Sardar K.M. Panikkar impresses that 'due to its earlier civilization and its predictable system of monsoon winds, it was the Indian Ocean region, and not the Mediterranean or Aegean Seas, which saw the world's first oceanic sailing activity. In his words, "*Millenniums before Columbus sailed the Atlantic and Magellan crossed the Pacific, Indian Ocean had become a thoroughfare of commercial and cultural traffic*". [1]

As a bridge between Asia and Europe, the Indian Ocean is not only a sign of rich history, but a global centre of trade and energy flow. It harbours more than half the world's container trade and 70 percent of petroleum shipments. Not just resources and trade, it is also the hub for geopolitical rivalry, piracy and maritime terrorism. It is third-largest of the world's five oceans and straddles Asia in the north, Africa in the west, Indo-China in the east, and Antarctica in the south. Home to four critical access waterways, the Suez Canal, Bab-el

Mandeb, the Strait of Hormuz and the Strait of Malacca, the Indian Ocean connects the Middle East, Africa and East Asia with Europe and the Americas. [2]

In the case of the Indian Ocean, many of the stakeholders are from outside the region. The EU, China, Japan and Korea are concerned about any disruptions to the Indian Ocean sea trade, which can impact their economies. The adaptation of a Chinese strategy of soft diplomacy in Asia and East Africa, along with the construction of new ports such as Hambantota and the Strings of Pearls Theory has raised concerns of a possible Chinese long-term plan to extend its sea power to the Indian Ocean. Likewise, it is believed that there are concerns raised by the Chinese about a U.S.-Indian strategic vision for the Asia Pacific and the Indian Ocean region. The other peculiarity of the Indian Ocean is the security threats that can emerge due to international terrorism. The most vulnerable points are the Straits of Hormuz and the Straits of Bab-el Mandeb, which remain key choke points for fossil fuel required by the global economy. [3] Ranil Wickremesinghe, Prime Minister of Sri Lanka at the Galle Dialogue 2015, opined,

"India's geographical location in the heart of the Indian Ocean makes it a vital player in the region. Whatever happens in the Indian Ocean will have a direct impact on India; hence Indian Ocean security is imminent for India. However, New Delhi considers Indian Ocean as its backyard and is never serious about the security".

For years, the New Delhi leadership has been trying to convince itself and the entire country that Pakistan is the only threat to India, and hence it has ignored strategically analysing threat from other regions. As early as 2004, late Mr. B. Raman warned that, "threat to us from Pakistan through Sri Lanka is more tactical than strategic, more subversive than military, more political than economic. China is a dragon, but Pakistan is still only a pinprick. We should be alert to the possibility of China and Pakistan acting in tandem with Sri Lanka and

Maldives to undermine the Indian influence, but there is as yet no evidence of this possibility becoming a reality, but it could be in the long-term. Our policy response should nip this bud before it starts blooming".

Despite this warning more than a decade ago, India took little steps to watch the growing Chinese and Pakistani presence in Sri Lanka and Maldives. In 2014, for the first time, the Government of India acknowledged that threat from South of India was severe than expected. However, India has done little to address these security challenges.

Not only politically, but also strategically as well as economically, China and Pakistan have started playing larger role in Sri Lanka and Maldives. Visit by the Chinese nuclear submarines to Sri Lanka; China gaining foothold in the Maldivian projects that was originally given to India; Pakistan appointing retired ISI officials as high commissioners in Sri Lanka and Maldives; and finally Pakistan engaging with the youth in both countries with the larger intentions of using them against India; it is a wonder that India despite taking note of the external influence, is procrastinating.

We have had a colonial legacy that defined the Indian Ocean as India's ocean. The reality is that India is an integral part of the Indian Ocean and any outside intrusion would have a direct impact on India. However, the Chinese do not feel so. One of the Chinese top naval officers Zhao Nanqi, former director of the General Logistics Department of the People's Liberation Army, proclaimed in 1993, "We can no longer accept the Indian Ocean as an ocean only of the Indians". Rightly or wrongly, Chinese presence in this region will have a direct impact on India's security and India cannot ignore or procrastinate.

This paper analyses major challenges to India's maritime security. It studies the reasons for external influence and the options India has to address these challenges. This paper also analyses non-traditional threats from South of India.

Is Maritime Threat Real?

The 26/11 attack on Mumbai was an eye opener for India's

strategic community, which until then did gave little credence to threat emerging from the sea. This more so, for New Delhi as for them, land borders between India and Pakistan were the only channel through which terrorists entered India. New Delhi never realised that the long coastline was as vulnerable, if not more, as the land borders. India has a coastline of about 7,517 kilometres. Composition includes nearly 5,423 kilometres along the mainland and 2,094 kilometres in the Andaman and Nicobar, and Lakshadweep Islands. The coastline mainly comprises of headlands, promontories, rocky shores, sandy spits, barrier beaches, open beaches, embayment, estuaries, inlets, bays, marshy land and offshore islands. [4]

India's long coastline is home to over 14.5 million people who are dependent on fishing sector directly and indirectly and who in the years have made India as the world's second largest producer of fish, contributing to 5.43 percent of the world fish production. This sector also happens to be a vital exporter, yielding over US$ 3.51 billion [5] for the Indian exchequer. The 9 coastal states and 2 union territories and 2 island states contribute more than 50 percent to the Indian GDP. Despite contributing significantly to the Indian economy, New Delhi has not shown major interest in enhancing the maritime security of the coastal states. Human trafficking, arrest of the Indian fishermen and other countries fishermen straying into the Indian coast, piracy, maritime terrorism, infiltration, etc., have been major sources of concern for Indian security and growth. The following sections highlight some of the major concerns in the Indian Ocean.

Indian Ocean as an International Zone

With an area of over 28,350,000 square miles, the Indian Ocean connects three important continents, namely Asia, Africa and Australia. Its southern region extends to the Antarctic Ocean and northern region does not go beyond the Tropic of Cancer. [6] The Indian Ocean constitutes a major junction of sea communication. For major countries like Australia, Britain,

China, France, India, Japan, the United States, Germany, etc., all their major supply lines of oil, foodstuff, and raw material pass through the Indian Ocean. [7]

The abundance of resource in the Indian Ocean has also made it vulnerable to conflict. History, time and again has proved that those who controlled the Indian Ocean ruled the world, hence the race to control Indian Ocean was also quite high. During the ancient period, the Chinese and South Asian kings; during the colonial period, the European colonial masters; during the Second World War, the Japanese and the Americans; during the Cold War, the British, Americans and Soviets; and finally the region witnesses the involvement of Americans, Chinese, Europeans and important Asian and other regional powers. This race among the external actors has increased competition among countries and has also made this region vulnerable for conflict not only in the maritime domain but also within the countries. Piracy in Somalia; ethnic conflict in African and Asia; religious extremism in the gulf region and the breeding of terrorism in the Indian Ocean bordering states are examples of vulnerability in this region.

Fear of external threat is not new; during the peak of Cold War between the U.S. and the USSR, in a statement issued by the U.S. Joint Chiefs of Staff in 1981 observed that 'The United States has a number of major interests in the region comprising the Middle East, the Persian Gulf, and the Northwest Indian Ocean. These interests involve access by the U.S. and its allies to the resources of the area, most notably oil from the Persian Gulf States—to include protection of transportation routes for the flow of that oil to North America, Western Europe and Japan…In the past year, the United States has taken a number of steps to improve the military balance in Southwest Asia. U.S. objectives call for a greater military presence, a capability to surge additional forces into the region, and access to facilities sufficient to support both peacetime presence and contingency operations…The United States has concluded agreements for use of support facilities in

Oman, Somalia and Kenya. Improvement of facilities in Diego Garcia is already under way'. [8]

The U.S. in addition to its base in Diego Garcia was also keen on taking over some of the islands in southern Maldives, namely Gan Island for recreation purpose of its soldiers. The Gan Islands was originally a British naval base that was established in 1941 during World War II. In early 1980s, the U.S. also attempted to establish Voice of America (VOA) tower in Sri Lanka but due to Indian pressure, this project did not materialise. However, VOA's presence has been felt since 2000.

The other super power during the Cold War, USSR was not far from establishing its presence in the Indian Ocean. According to S. Koslov, the Novosti Press military correspondent asserted that in view of its geographical position, the USSR needs a large fleet in order to maintain the necessary internal contacts with remote parts of the country. Vitally important communication routes linking the European with Asiatic and Far Eastern parts of the USSR pass through the Mediterranean and across the Indian Ocean. It is quite clear that the existing land routes cannot be any substitute for these more economic and convenient sea routes. [9]

The Soviet Union also maintained a large network of "mooring buoys" and submarines all over the Indian Ocean as rendezvous points for its warships. Adding to these assets in the Indian Ocean, the 1971 Indo-Soviet Friendship Treaty enabled frequent visits of the Soviet Union's ships to the Indian ports. It is also believed that one of the prime movers for Soviet Union's 1979 war on Afghanistan was to gain access to the Indian Ocean. [10]

Since the end of Cold War, the race for dominance in the Indian Ocean has increased. One of the important players in the present scenario who is likely to play a larger role, and also replace the role played by the erstwhile Soviet Union is the Chinese. While Soviet Union's race for dominance was short-lived, for the Chinese, it is more like a return to the age old glory.

Maritime Silk Route (MSR) and One Belt, One Road (OBOR)

In the 21st Century, the international community witnessed many financial aids given by the developed nations for development and also for strategic reasons of the developing as well as the affected countries and regions. The best example being The Marshal Plan provided by the U.S. to retain Europe as one unit. The Chinese are a new entrant into this game. OBOR is the Chinese manifestation for a larger global role. The international opinion is divided among the countries who intended to receive support from the Chinese and countries who fear that China's role could make them permanently indebted. In the eyes of those countries who see China as a competitor, the OBOR gives the impression of a direct counter measure to the twin challenges of the U.S. rebalancing policy knows as the "pivot to Asia" and the Chinese's own economic slowdown. [11]

The Concept of New Silk Road is an initiative that is close to President Xi Jinping. He proposed this major initiative in two important and significant speeches. First, at Nazarbayev University at Kazakhastan on September 7, 2013 on the modern Silk Road Economic Belt and followed by the announcement on "Maritime Silk Road" at a speech at the Indonesian Parliament on October 3, 2013. These two speeches marked a major game changer in the international arena.

According to the Chinese government, the Maritime Silk Road would connect and replicate their ancient Silk Road. The MSR would support China to regain all their lost grounds in the Indian Ocean. Starting from reasserting their hold on the East and South China Sea, China has expanded its influence in Pacific, South Asia, West Asia, Eastern and Southern Africa.

Chinese role in South Asia has been significant as except for India, Bhutan and Nepal, other countries have become partners to the Chinese MSR initiative. As a result, Chinese investments have multiplied in less than a decade. While the Chinese projects in South Asia on the face may look like economic investments, a significant number of these projects are strategically important to establish a foot hold in the Indian Ocean. The Chinese interests in Sri Lanka and Maldives is significant as both these countries are geographically located closer to the International Sea Lines of Communication and any disturbance to the current balance in the Indian Ocean would have drastic effects on India's growth and security.

It is estimated that Sri Lanka has received over US$ 4 billion since 2009. Their investments in Sri Lanka include:

- Hambantota Port and Industrial Complex: US$ 1 billion.
- Mattala Rajapaksa International Airport: US$ 210 million.
- Container terminal at the Colombo Port: US$ 500 million.
- Colombo-Katunayake Expressway: US$ 248 million.
- Improvement of the railways: US$ 100 million.
- Norochcholai Coal Power Plant: US$ 855 million.
- A flood protection system for Colombo suburbs of Kotte, Dehiwela-Mount Lavinia, Maharagama, Kesbewa and Moratuwa: US$ 59 million.
- National Theatre of Performing Arts in Colombo: US$ 21 million.
- Lotus Tower in Colombo: US$ 100 million.

Of these, four projects namely the Hambantota Port, Mattala Airport, Colombo Port and the Lotus Tower in Colombo are likely to play a dual role of both supporting Sri Lankan growth as well as gathering intelligence for the China. Visit of the two Chinese submarines in 2014 is a good illustration of how China would use their overseas investments its advantage. Two submarines, first diesel powered "Great Wall No. 329" along with the support ship "Changxing Island" and nuclear powered "Changzheng-2" along with a PLA Navy (PLAN) escort warship "Chang Xing Dao" were docked in Colombo from September 7 to 14, 2014 and November 6, 2014 respectively.

These visits raised alarms in New Delhi, which immediately conveyed its concerns to Sri Lanka. While after the first visit of the submarines, Sri Lanka tried to assure India that this visit would not compromise India's security concerns and that it would keep India abreast of any further visits, however, during the second visit of the nuclear submarine, Sri Lanka deliberately ignored informing New Delhi. Sri Lankan Petroleum Industries Minister Anura P. Yapa's address to the media that "the government would not be having talks with India on this issue" was not only a violation of the Indo-Sri Lankan Accord of 1987 but also a deliberate attempt to ignore New Delhi's concern. [12]

Considering that these visits would have a limited impact on India's security, what is actually worrying is the construction of the Lotus Tower by the two Chinese companies, namely the China National Electronic Import and Export Corporation (CNEIEC) and the Chinese Aerospace Long-March International Trade (CALMIT). These companies are not regular civil construction firms but are involved in defence electronics system integration, construction of defence electronics system, integration of public security responding to international anti-terrorism, defence equipment, technology and services, export of anti-terrorism and anti-riot equipment, technologies and services among other activities. [13] With the technological advancement, any surveillance facility can be hidden from the naked eyes.

Not just in Sri Lanka, China has also made inroads into Maldives. The Maldivian Government headed by President Abdulla Yameen has awarded the US$800 million contract for expansion of the Maldivian Airport to the Chinese firm 'Beijing Urban Construction Group'. This project was originally contracted to GMR, an Indian firm. This contract came to a sudden halt in 2012 due to political reasons and GMR was not only forcefully sent out but also without any proper compensation. Even the arbitration between Maldivian Government and the GMR at Singapore did not result favourably for GMR. Chinese inroad into Sri Lanka and Maldives is working against India's security interest and New Delhi continues to be ignorant of its long-term impact.

Fundamentalism and Maritime Threat

Since the early 1980s, maritime terrorism in the Indian Ocean was often related to the activities of the LTTE (Liberation Tigers of Tamil Eelam). Be it smuggling, piracy, suicide attack on ships etc., were seen as LTTE's operation. Although, since 2009, the situation has changed in Sri Lanka and LTTE has been vanquished and the armed conflict has ended, yet the threat remains. So is LTTE the only challenge in this region? Terrorism since the U.S. war on Afghanistan in 2001 is more related to terrorism, promulgated by the religious fundamental groups. Al-Qaeda, ISIS and ISIL, and other fundamental groups operating out of Indian Ocean Region are all eyeing at disruption of Sea Lines of Communication as an important tool in furthering their agenda. Two illustrations to explain the growth of extremism in the South of Indian region are outlined below.

Firstly, while the ISI operatives working in Sri Lanka have always been subtle, since 2004, both Sri Lanka and Pakistan have started openly advocating ISI's role in Sri Lanka, especially in Ampara and Puttalam, which are in eastern and western parts of Sri Lanka respectively. Strategic expert, Late Mr. B. Raman as early as 2004, cautioned the Indian government about the appointment of Colonel (Retd.) Bashir Wali as the Pakistani Ambassador to Sri Lanka. For Colonel Wali, this was the second posting in the Pakistani High Commission in Colombo. He had earlier served as the head of the Pakistani intelligence set up in the High Commission in the 1990s. It was during his previous stay in Colombo that Al-Ummah, expanded its activities in Tamil Nadu and Kerala.

It was also found that Colonel Wali was an active member of the Tablighi Jamaat and was instrumental in a number of Tamil Muslims from the Eastern Province studying in the Binori madrasa at Karachi on scholarships provided by the Tablighi Jamaat. This practice is carried out even now. In 2012, the Sri Lankan government expelled nearly 151 preachers belonging to the Tablighi Jamaat. Has this expulsion saved Sri Lanka from being influenced by the extremists? Rather, the flow of preachers from Pakistan and Saudi has only increased. Colombo continues to patronise these preachers to appease Pakistan.

Secondly, recently in Maldives, a country that is 100 percent Sunni Muslim country, all the mosques are controlled by the government. The decision to permit the religious group Tablighi Jamaat to preach in the Maldives has caused controversy, with some members of the public walking out of mosques in protest. The Adaalath Party (right wing conservative party) openly defended the Tablighi Jamaat members visiting the Maldives. Despite concerns being raised by a moderate section of the society, the government has allowed members of the Tablighi Jamaat to speak at various mosques—I am afraid fundamentalism has gained enough grounds in the peripheral areas of Maldives.

I should also impress that some of the Maldivians who were trained by the LeT and Taliban were recently arrested in Kerala. These groups are working towards setting up their centres in Kerala and Tamil Nadu. During the presentation, recently at the seminar organised by a Jamaat, the author mentioned that the extremists/terrorists can enter south of India with the support of fishermen and one of the participants, openly countered it by saying that "infiltration was an open secret and the government agencies are well aware of it. However, the Government of India and Tamil Nadu were too busy solving major issues, and infiltration and terrorism are minor concerns".

Conclusion

Relations between India, Sri Lanka, and Maldives have always been asymmetrical. Mainly due to geography and demography, Sri Lanka and Maldives fear that any cooperation with India would only lead to the big brother taking an upper hand and not an equal partnership. In fact, there is a strong accusation that SAARC should not become a 'shark association', wherein India might swallow its smaller neighbours instead of jointly working towards ending any issue. It is this fear that makes our southern neighbours get themselves involved in activities that can endanger them as well as India. Refuelling of Pakistani flights in Sri Lanka in 1971 is a good illustration to explain the complicity of southern neighbours' relations with India.

During the East Pakistani crisis, India withdrew landing and over-flying facilities to the Pakistani International Airlines (PIA). To the shock and dismay of the Indian observers, Sri Lanka granted refuelling facilities for Pakistani aircrafts on their way to East Pakistan to carry on savage reprisals against the Bangladeshi nationalists. In March 1971, 16 east bound and 15 west bound Pakistani Air Force planes landed at Katunayake airport. While Sri Lanka denied providing such facilities, Indian writers, especially Late K. Subrahmaniam, India's foremost defence analyst, has maintained that these flights involved plain clothed Pakistani soldiers and war materials.

A 26/11 style attack in any of the southern states, would leave a human fatality running in thousands. The 2015 floods in Chennai and the 2016 attack on Pathankot showed to the world the poor disaster management of the Government of India and the state governments. Despite the Navy, Coastguard and the Army getting into action, lack of coordination by the Government of Tamil Nadu led to a huge disaster. If this was the response to natural disasters, a terrorist attack in any of the southern city, would bring about irreparable disaster. It is time the government of the day takes adequate measures to prevent security challenges emerging from the Indian Ocean.

Endnotes

1. Admiral (Retd.) Arun Prakash, "Maritime Security of India: Future Challenges", keynote speech at the Y.B. Chavan memorial talk, organised by Institute for Defence Studies and Analysis on November 26, 2013, available at: http://www.idsa.in/keyspeeches/MaritimeSecurityOfIndiaFuture

Challenges.
2. Harsh V. Pant, "India in the Indian Ocean: Growing Mismatch between Ambitions and Capabilities", *Pacific Affairs*, Vol. 82, No. 2, Summer, 2009.
3. Speech by Ranil Wickremesinghe, Prime Minister of Sri Lanka at the Galle Dialogue 2015 on November 23, 2015, available at: http://slemb.ph/keynote-address-delivered-by-hon-ranil-wickremesinghe-prime-minister-at-galle-dialogue-2015-on-monday-23rd-november-2015-3.
4. V. Sanil Kumar, et al., "Coastal Processes Along the Indian Coastline", *Current Science*, Vol. 91, No. 4, August 25, 2006, available at: http://www.iisc.ernet.in/~currsci/aug252006/530.pdf.
5. "National Aquaculture Sector Overview: India", Food and Agriculture Organization of the United Nations, available at: http://www.fao.org/fishery/countrysector/naso_india.
6. Chandra Kumar, "The Indian Ocean: Arc of Crisis or Zone of Peace?", *International Affairs,* Royal Institute of International Affairs, Vol. 60, No. 2, Spring, 1984, p. 235.
7. B. Vivekanandan, "The Indian Ocean as a Zone of Peace: Problems and Prospects", *Asian Survey*, Vol. 21, No. 12, December 1981, p. 1239.
8. Quoted in Namboodiri, Anand and Sridhar, "Intervention in the Indian Ocean", New Delhi: ABC, 1982, pp. 159-60. Excerpts published in the book are taken from *USICA Backgrounder*, February 7, 1981 in Chandra Kumar, "The Indian Ocean: Arc of Crisis or Zone of Peace?", *International Affairs,* Royal Institute of International Affairs, Vol. 60, No. 2, Spring, 1984, p. 234.
9. B. Vivekanandan, "The Indian Ocean as a Zone of Peace: Problems and Prospects", *Asian Survey*, Vol. 21, No. 12, December 1981, p. 1237.
10. David Brewster, "India's Ocean: The Story of India's Bid for Regional Leadership", Abingdon, Oxon: Routledge, 2014.
11. Gan Junxian and Mao Yan, "China's New Silk Road: Where Does It Lead?", *Asian Perspective*, 40, No. 1, 2016, available at: http://www.questia.com/read/1P3-3957054031/china-s-new-silk-road-where-does-it-lead.
12. Col. R. Hariharan, "Security Concerns over Chinese Submarines Visit to Colombo", *South Asia Analysis Group,* Paper No. 5818, November 10, 2014 available at:

http://www.southasiaanalysis.org/node/1650.

13. Ashik Bonofer, "Sri Lanka 2015: Benchmark or Landmark for Change" in Vijay Sakhuja (ed.), *South Asia Defence and Strategic Perspective*, Pentagon Press: New Delhi, 2016, p. 162.

6

India's Coastal Security: A Perspective

Suresh R.

The concept of security has various dimensions. During the Cold War period, threat to security of a nation was mainly from the other nation states. However, in the post-Cold War era, the threat to national security emanates from the non-state actors. There are some non-traditional threats to national security including international terrorism. This new threat can be addressed only with the active support of other nation states as well as people. Similarly, in the post-Cold War period, human security issues have assumed great significance. Thus, it is the responsibility of a nation to address both national security and human security issues simultaneously. Interestingly, the coastal security is an area where the national security and human security interests converge.

India's coastal security has become an urgent necessity especially in the context of the Mumbai terrorist attacks and also the recent attempt by terrorists to enter from Porbander off the coast of Gujarat and the threat it poses to the national security. In the post-Cold War period, the threat to the security of nation states emanates mainly from non-state actors. Unlike the attack from state actors, the non-state actor's mode of attack is different. It demands a constant vigil throughout the land and maritime borders.

The Italian Marine issues added a new dimension to the security of the coastal people engaged in fishing. This paper is an attempt to examine the coastal security dimension regards India's national security, especially in the context of porous coastal area of 7,516 kilometres along the Indian coastline.

Security: The Changing Dimensions

With the end of the Cold War, the concept of security has increasingly come under scrutiny from scholars of international relations. In the classical formulation, security is about how nation states use force to manage threats to their territorial integrity, their autonomy, and their domestic political order, primarily from other nation states. This classical national security formulation has been criticized on various grounds. A nation may be secure from the external military threat but that does not mean all people living in that nation are secure. The social, economic and political orders prevalent in a nation have an implication on the security of the people. Thus, the source of threat to the security of the people is not solely from other nations' defence forces but also from within the nation. The system of government prevalent, the standard of living, and the rights enjoyed by the people have a bearing on the security of people as well as security of the nations. Thus, the main referent of security includes not only the nation states but also the people living in the state.

The debates on security in the post-Cold War period is cantered mainly on the pre-suppositions about what security is, what is being secured, the causes of insecurity, and how best to address insecurity. International relations theorists and policy experts have varying perspectives on these questions, which have evolved and have had changing levels of acceptance over time. Realists and neo-realists emphasise nation state as the central referent of security, both as the lens through which security is understood, as well as the tool by which security is best maintained or restored. Liberal theorists recognize a wider set of values embedded in the concept of the state and state security, in the methods and means to address insecurity, and the actors involved.

The critical constructivist scholars understand that the interests and identities of nation states are themselves constructed by the distribution of ideas and interests within the state-based system and this shapes a state's security interests and how these are conceived, and in turn impacts upon the actions necessary to ensure security. Thus, there are divergent views with regard to concept of security, whose security—that is whether the security of the nation or people—the causes of insecurity, and how to ensure security.

The Westphalia state system had made nation states as the basic unit in the international system—and that nation states are sovereign and independent. Each nation decides their internal and external policies. The prime responsibility of a nation state is to promote its national interests. The national interests of nation states are mainly to ensure peace, security and prosperity. However, they differ with regard to the means adopted to achieve these national interests. Some nations employ aggressive means and some peaceful methods. And foreign policy of a nation is the means to achieve their respective national interests. Therefore, though the national interests of nation states are similar, nations frame divergent foreign policy, which in turn is conditioned by the interplay of internal and external factors. Thus, the foreign policy changes occur in accordance with the transformations in the internal and external conditions. Concomitantly, the security policy of nations also changes.

It appears that in the post-Cold War global system, threat to security of people and nation states emanates largely from non-traditional sources. In this context, the classical security paradigm which is based solely on military security fails to address the non-traditional security issues. This again demands a new approach to security in order to address the non-traditional threats which are not purely military in nature. Again, since most of the non-traditional threats to security are transnational in nature, they demand a multilateral effort from the nation states.

The conceptual shift that has occurred after the end of the Cold War is that security can be dealt with through cooperation rather than confrontation. Since the threat to the security of nations is not mainly from the threat posed by the military of other nations, the existence of non-traditional threats along with the transnational nature of these threats has necessitated cooperation of nation states on security matters. At present no nation, whatsoever powerful is in a position to resolve these security problems single-handedly. All these factors point to need for cooperation of nations on security related issues.

However, the cooperation in security matters depends upon mutual trust, transparency, acceptance of global norms and relinquishing Cold War-based military power dominance and zero-sum approach to security. It requires a broader look at the concept of national interest. In order to address non-traditional security threats, dialogue, transparency, information sharing, capacity building, and confidence building measures are significant means. Again track-II diplomacy assumes great significance in information sharing in the age of information and communication technology. Along with the government, the civil society organizations are also required to play a dominant role in international relations.

Another notable feature with regard to security is that since the Cold War, the concept of security has become more and more institutionalized. At the national level, each nation possesses military power to meet any threat to its national security from other nation states. Similarly, at the international level, the United Nations Security Council is mandated to maintain international peace and security even by adopting coercive means. The international mechanism established to meet the challenges to world peace in the aftermath of the Second World War has become defunct to address the 21st century global problems. This is not only because of the changes in the nature of security threats but also due to the lack of representations to nations with high quantity of human resources in the global governance. It is essential to initiate democratic governance at the international level.

The existing international institutions are less capable of mitigating the global challenges posed by climate change, water, food, and energy security. Similarly, the growing significance of non-state actors which are more powerful than the nation states in terms of resources and area of operation also demand new international regulatory mechanism. The domestic and international institutions need to further evolve and develop mechanisms to engage each other more adequately, in order to be better equipped to deal with these global challenges.

Thus, in the 21st century, the states are confronted with a number of new security challenges which necessitates a change in the way the states approach these challenges. As a result of the impact of globalization and consequently more interconnectedness of the world, any change in one part of the world affects the other. State failures are increasing as a result of ongoing globalization process which also poses a threat to the security of the nation as well as the people. In this context, it is necessary to define what constitutes a security issue today. Scholars have found that classical frameworks are not easily adapted to the contemporary security landscape since there exists a blurred boundary between human security and national security on the one hand and the national security and international security on the other.

India's Maritime Security Interests

India has a coastline of 7,516 kilometres and the territorial limit extends to 12 nautical miles from the coast and exclusive economic zone (EEZ) of 200 nautical miles, which covers 2 million square kilometres. There are nine States and four Union Territories that have coastal area. Though it is the duty of the Indian navy and the Indian Coast Guard to provide the security of the maritime borders, they cannot keep a constant vigil on the movement of men and materials along the entire coastal region. The Indian navy is mainly stationed to the area beyond 200 nautical miles in international waters and Indian Coast Guard to look after the area from 12 nautical miles up to 200 nautical miles and the coastal police is responsible for the area up to 12 nautical miles from the shore. Therefore, coastal policing is necessary to supplement and not supplant the security responsibility of the Indian defence forces. It is also important to note that coastal policing through coastal police stations alone cannot ensure a foolproof security arrangement in the coastal area or through the construction of fencing along the coastal area. Therefore, the cooperation and support of the coastal community is sine qua non for the coastal security.

India has to step up surveillance and protection of India's vast coastline of 7,516 kilometres. India's maritime zones, over which it has certain rights and obligations, include a territorial sea up to 12 nautical miles (22 kilometres) from the baseline, a contiguous zone from 12 to 24 nautical miles (22-44 kilometres), an exclusive economic zone (EEZ) from 12 to 200 nautical miles (22-370 kilometres) and a continental shelf up to 200 nautical miles.

These zones currently comprise 2.013 million square kilometres area of sea which is the 12th largest in the world and equivalent to two-thirds of the total land area. India has thousand-plus island territories and offshore installations. Again, since nearly 70 percent of India's energy requirements of crude oil are currently shipped from abroad, an increased focus would be required on the ability to maintain the safety and security of energy shipments and the prevention of any disruption of supply through multilateral cooperation. Another important maritime security interest of India is the prevention of maritime terrorism not only through multilateral efforts but also through comprehensive coastal security programme with the involvement of the coastal community.

The task of providing security to the vast coastline, unlike the land borders, is a complex phenomenon involving multiple stake holders such as shipping, fisheries, offshore exploration and production, tourism, and scientific community. It is not only important to protect and promote the multifarious interests of different stake holders but also involve them in the coastal security programme.

Coastal Security and Maritime Security Agencies

There are nine states and four union territories that have coastal area. Though it is the duty of the Indian navy and the Indian coast guard to provide the security of the maritime borders they cannot keep a constant vigil on the movement of men and material along the entire coastal region. There is currently a fragmentation of organizations, policies and legal and enforcement measures relating to maritime security issues. This results in overlapping of jurisdiction and inability to provide quick decisions or respond effectively to fast evolving situations. Currently, as many as 12 ministries and eight departments of the central government are involved in maritime-related policy formulation and implementation, as are nine coastal states and four union territories, with defence left to the Indian Navy and the Indian Coast Guard.

To deal with such a situation, a formal mechanism for coordination among the multiple users of the sea is urgently required. This would enable effective and time-urgent coordination among varied maritime related ministries and departments of the Government, as also the concerned states and union territories. In this respect, the Group of Ministers' report has recommended the formation of "an apex body for management of maritime affairs". Such an apex body would coordinate the activities of various agencies operating from different regions and having different mandates. The coastal security scheme is one such comprehensive initiative to address the problem of coastal security with the involvement of the coastal community.

Coastal Security Schemes and the Role of Coastal Community

The Coastal Security Scheme has been formulated for strengthening the infrastructure for patrolling and surveillance of country's coastal areas, particularly the shallow areas close to the coast to check and counter illegal cross-border activities and criminal activities using the coast or sea. The Ministry of Home Affairs has been implementing Coastal Security Scheme in two phases (Phase-I: 2005 to 2011 and Phase-II: 2011 to 2015). The scheme also aims at establishing institutional arrangements at state and district level for coordination among various agencies including the Indian Coast Guard and the Indian Navy.

The Coastal Security Scheme is under implementation in the nine coastal States and four coastal Union Territories since 2005. Under the scheme, in the first phase (2005-2011) assistance has been given to all the coastal states of Gujarat, Maharashtra, Goa, Karnataka, Kerala, Tamil Nadu, Andhra Pradesh, Odisha and West Bengal and the Union Territories of Daman and Diu, Lakshadweep, Puducherry and Andaman and Nicobar Islands to set up 73 coastal police stations, 97 check posts, and 58 outposts. Under Phase-II (2011 to 2015) of the Scheme, it has been proposed to provide 131 marine police stations, 60 jetties, and 10 marine operation centres.

The proposal of the Phase-II Coastal Security Scheme has been formulated on the basis of vulnerability/gap analysis carried out by the coastal States and Union Territories in consultation with the Indian Coast Guard. The proposal was approved by the Government of India on September 24, 2010 for implementation from April 1, 2011 for a period of five years. The Scheme has provided support to coastal States/Union Territories to upgrade their coastal security apparatus. Nevertheless the task of securing India's vast coastline is immense. There are 12 major ports and around 200 minor ports in the country. The 12 major ports are International Ship and Port Facility Security (ISPS) compliant and are subject to security audit once in two years. However, there is no such mechanism of security audit for the non-major ports. Apart from 12 major ports, 53 minor/non-major ports and 5 shipyards in the country are ISPS compliant.

As per the report of the Ministry of Home Affairs in India, a three-tier coastal security ring all along India's coast is provided by the Marine Police, Indian Coast Guard and Indian Navy. Extensive surveillance and patrolling has been put into place across the Eastern and Western coastlines by the security forces in a co-ordinated manner. The Indian Coast Guard is undertaking extensive patrolling and surveillance along the eastern and western coast in coordination with other Central and State agencies viz. Indian Navy, Marine Police, Customs, CISF, Port Authority etc.

Further, for effective surveillance, the deployment of assets by Indian Coast Guard in the Exclusive Economic Zone has been enhanced. On an average, every day about 18-20 ICG Ships are on patrol whereas about 8-10 aircrafts are on aerial surveillance sortie. At least one ship is being maintained on maritime borders with Pakistan and Sri Lanka. In addition, waters off Lakshadweep and Minicoy islands are maintained under constant surveillance during non-monsoon period by deployment of assets alternatively by the Indian Coast Guard and the Indian Navy.

Recent Coastal Security Initiatives

The Indian Navy in its 2015 Report maintained that strengthening of maritime security including offshore and coastal security is a multi-stakeholder activity, and measures continue to be implemented by various Ministries/agencies. These measures broadly include induction of assets, recruitment of additional manpower, development of infrastructure, improving information exchange mechanisms, and addressing gaps in the existing systems.

With regard to inter-agency coordination, the Report claimed that continued efforts towards greater inter-agency coordination at all levels have resulted in an increased coordination and cooperation amongst all stakeholders. A National Command, Control, Communication and Information (NC3I) Network interconnecting 51 Naval and Coast Guard stations has been established to develop a common operational picture (COP) between the two agencies. The network will integrate inputs from the chain of static sensors, 6 stations of the National AIS Chain, Long Range Identification System (LRIT) and information from open sources.

The maritime forces available for coastal security include armed forces and other maritime forces. The Sagar Prahari Bal has been raised by the Indian Navy for force protection, security of naval bases and vital assets and points. Towards strengthening offshore security, immediate support vessels have been procured for patrolling of the offshore development area.

Role of Coastal Community in Coastal Security

Indian Coast Guard is regularly conducting community interaction programmes in the fishing villages along the coasts. The community interaction programmes are aimed at sensitizing the fishing community on the prevailing security situation and develop them to be the 'eyes and ears' for intelligence gathering. It was started in 2009, and a total of 1919 community interaction programmes have been conducted by the Indian Coast Guard. Thus, the security agencies have well accepted the role of the coastal community in the coastal security scheme.

Again on May 15, 2013, Defence Minister of India called upon various agencies to work together to ensure a seamless and robust coastal security architecture and stated that fishermen should be made an integral part of the security planning. He also said that an integrated approach was essential for a strong coastal security and noted that fishermen were the "eyes and ears" for overall coastal security. However, so far the involvement of coastal community in coastal security scheme is limited to sensitizing them through periodic awareness programme undertaken by Indian Coast Guard and Marine police.

In this connection, the proposal put forth by Professor K.R. Singh is an innovative step to gain the support of the coastal community in coastal security programme on a permanent basis. He had suggested the setting up of marine guards on the lines of home guards by recruiting coastal people from each coastal locality. These trained marine guards would help the coastal security agencies in intelligence gathering which is a very vital input for the coastal security agencies to monitor the movement of men and material along the vast coastal area. The gathering of intelligence through human beings would also support the surveillance through electronic gadgets.

This proposal if implemented will not only help to solve unemployment among the coastal people but would also help to enlist the support and cooperation of the coastal community in security related activities on a permanent basis. It is important to note that Karnataka State has already selected 200 fishermen to be employed in coastal security police. The people from coastal villages can be recruited in the marine police force as marine guards and their seafaring experience is likely to be an asset for the security agencies.

In addition, the coastal people can be trained to gather information which would support and supplement the necessary intelligence inputs for the marine police. India has a long coastal stretch and at several places the stretch lacks security forces. Hence, the fishermen if trained, can be used to alert and inform in case they find anything unusual such as a person photographing or sketching, contacting ships with torch signals, transferring goods from a ship to a boat, transferring people, fisher folk fishing in areas not meant for fishing and are acting suspiciously or people urging fisher folk in buying their boats or renting them by paying a huge amount of money. One of the major problems with the new recruits in marine police is that they do not know the local language. Therefore, it is necessary to concentrate on area-wise recruitment for marine police. And through periodic awareness programme, the coastal community can be trained to gather vital intelligence inputs for the security agencies. Thus, when it came to protecting the coastal borders of the country, the fishing community could play a big role. In fact, every sea-faring fisherman can be trained to be a front man for coastal security.

The Triton mock-drill, a coastal security exercise

conducted by the Indian Navy had shown that terrorists could still find passages into the country through the sea. It has been pointed out that at one instance during the Triton exercise, "enemies" sent through the sea by the security agencies could bribe and gain entry into the country at one or two points. Therefore, there should be more awareness on coastal security. During this exercise, it was also found that certain coastal areas remained vigilant and the "terrorists" were captured with the cooperation of the fishing community. It shows that sea-faring fishermen were the eyes and ears of coastal security and no amount of modernised coastal security measures would equal them. As part of the coastal security programme, it had been decided to equip all categories of fishing vessels with radio-frequency identification gadgets. It would enable the security agencies to identify each and every fishing vessel out in sea. This, in turn, would enable checking of vessels without the gadget. Even then, the fishing community would continue to be a vital aspect of coastal security.

The task of providing security to the vast coastline, unlike the land borders, is a complex phenomenon involving multiple stake holders. Among these stake holders, the role of coastal community assumes significance in the coastal security programme. They are considered as eyes and ears of the coastal security. Now the question arises as to how to enlist the cooperation and support of the coastal community for effective coastal policing. Such support and cooperation is necessary on a permanent basis and round the clock. The cooperation and support of the coastal people is needed day in and day out to ensure coastal security. The livelihood for the fishing community comes from the sea. In this connection, they also require protection from the security agencies involved in anti-piracy and related security operations of the defence forces.

In order to ensure the support of the coastal community, it is important to build a better coastal community-police relations. Unlike other areas, a coastal area is mainly occupied by the fishing community. Their problems are different from the problems of the people living in other area. Generally, the coastal areas lag behind in basic amenities. This includes lack of safe drinking water, sanitation, proper housing, education, and other infrastructural facilities such as roads, hospitals, markets etc.

Since the livelihoods of the coastal community come from fishing, it is difficult to replace the coastal area settlers. The whole hearted cooperation and support of the coastal community can be ensured only by improving the living conditions of the coastal people. The coastal community faces natural calamities such as sea erosion, tsunami etc. They are also victims of climate change, pollution, and poverty. In short, the human security issues are numerous and imminent as far as the coastal community is concerned.

Thus, when we look into the coastal security, a convergence of the national security concerns and human security concerns is visible. The overall development of the coastal area would lead to better human security and better human security would result in enlisting the support of the coastal community in national security programme. Thus, the development of infrastructural facilities in the coastal area not only improves the human security but also enhances the coastal and the maritime security.

The security agencies in India had already maintained that the coastal community is vital for the coastal security. It is this understanding on the part of the security agencies which led to formal interaction between the coastal communities and the security agencies. The mass awareness drive has been initiated by the Indian Coast Guard in association with the Department of Fisheries at various locations. The main objective of the drive was to re-emphasize the responsibility of the fishing community towards the coastal security setup and their role as "eyes and ears" of the security agencies. This programme was also utilized to educate fishermen on safety and security aspects while operating at sea. Such interactions are beneficial for both the security agencies and the fishing community. It also enhances better police community relationship.

Again, the coastal security projects have also envisaged the construction of coastal roads along the coastal areas and the development of infrastructural facilities. Such development along the coastal area would also promote coastal (beach) tourism. The development of tourism along the coastal area would also enhance the employment opportunities for the coastal people. One of the major problems before the coastal community is unemployment. This problem can be well addressed by the development of tourism along the coastal areas.

Thus, particular attention needs to be paid to the maritime dimensions of national security as it is closely linked to India's political stability and economic prosperity. Concomitantly, in maritime security, the coastal security aspect needs to be focused. Along with enhancing the operational capabilities of the security agencies, the problems of the coastal community also need to be addressed. A comprehensive programme needs to be initiated to address all the aspects of coastal security with the active support of the coastal community. And the investments in the coastal security with the involvement of coastal people will not only enhance the national security but will also augment human security.

References

Annual Reports of the Ministry of Home Affairs, Government of India, 2005-2015.

Annual Reports of the Ministry of External Affairs, Government of India, 2005-2015.

Annual Reports of the Ministry of Defence, Government of India, 2005-2015.

"India's Maritime Military Strategy", Ministry of Defence, Government of India, New Delhi. Also see, "The Indian Navy's Vision Document", May 2006, available at: www.indiannavy.nic.in.

Singh, K.R. (2013), "Coastal Security: Maritime Dimensions of India's Homeland Security", Vij Publications, New Delhi.

Suresh, R. (2012), "Peace in the Indian Ocean: A South Asian

Perspective", Serials Publications, New Delhi.

Suresh, R. (2013), "India's Security Policy in the Post-Cold War Period", in Mohanan B Pillai (ed.), 'India's National Security: Concerns and Strategies', New Century Publications, New Delhi.

Suresh, R. (2006), "Human Security: A Canadian Perspective", *Holistic Thought*, Volume V, Nos. 1 and 2, January-December, pp. 103-113.

Suresh, R. (2014), "Maritime Security of India: The Coastal Security Challenges and Policy Options", Vij Books India Pvt. Ltd., New Delhi.

7

Challenges to Indian Defence Co-operation with Russia

Zeeshan Munir

India has traversed a long journey of bilateral relations with Russia. In the historical context, it has passed through different phases of introduction, evolution, expansion and challenges. Since India's Independence, Russia has closely cooperated to the needs of the Indian armed forces. This cooperation grew wide enough to provide a solid base for the Indian defence forces. Thus, over the years, India emerged as the leading importer of Russian military hardware in the world. This further helped in building a unique trust between the two nations wherein Russia lined its cutting edge military technologies which it otherwise denied to other nations. This flow of Russian arms helped India several times to counter threats to its territory and maintain its military strength.

However, this unique defence cooperation was defenceless to the new challenges which emerged domestically in both the nations. The 1990s saw the Indian foray to economic liberalization, while Soviet Russia disintegrated. This altered an otherwise exceptional friendship, bringing in new challenges. Further, India drifted towards U.S. and also expanded its defence imports. These new scenarios challenged the monopoly of Russian defence market in India. Various irritants started creeping in into the robust Indo-Russian defence cooperation. At the same time, official stance has always projected the need for maintaining this close cooperation.

Thus, this paper will first attempt to provide a historical

framework of the Indo-Russian cooperation and how the defence component fits in the overall relations. It will also discuss the various mechanisms of their defence cooperation. At the end, this paper will try to address the key challenges of Indo-Russian defence cooperation in the present context of Indian aspirations and Russian pragmatism.

Strengthening Defence Cooperation

Strengthening defence cooperation with friendly foreign countries is an important component of our national security and defence strategy (Defense, 2013-14).

India in the 21st century has emerged as a major Asian power with aspirations for playing greater role in the international politics. Since its Independence, it steadfastly created a strong defence force which has faced more than three conventional wars and is involved in counter-insurgency within its borders, besides safeguarding its geopolitical interests beyond its borders. Thus, in pursuit of India's defence requirements, the cooperation and help provided by Russia cannot be ignored. The defence aid from Soviet Russia had two underlying uniqueness.

First, it was Soviet Russia which provided the initial thrust that was required to build up India's military capability even when in international politics the intensity of Cold War was at its peak. Second, it was also when India had declared itself not to be part of any rival camps during the Cold War era. The Soviet military help was instrumental in making India grow militarily and also as a regional power. These defence aids from Soviet Russia thus helped in the foundation of a very different sort of relation between the two nations that was based on mutual trust and cooperation. This relation was broadened with supporting each other in international politics too. This closeness between the two countries was the result of several changing circumstances in international as well as domestic arena in respective countries that required them to carve out the foundation of their relations.

However, the collapse of the Soviet Union and subsequent end of Cold War completely changed the dynamics and conduct of international relations. This too had a cast on the otherwise strong relations between India and Soviet Russia. The end of bi-polarity and increased economic liberalization and globalization gave way to new challenges and re-orientation of relations among different nations. This post-1990s world order also steered India's policies thus setting its priorities away from the intense ideological rivalry of Cold War. India started diversification of its defence imports.

This diversification brought in new players in the billion dollar Indian defence market and countering the large share of Russian defence exports to India. Not of recently, U.S. emerged as the largest exporter of arms to India, thereby necessitating the Indian arms procurement policy to balance between the erstwhile Cold War rivals i.e. the U.S. and Russia (Pandit, 2015).

Let us discuss the *historical framework of Indo-Russian cooperation in general and Indo-Russian defence cooperation in particular.* We will then very briefly detail the present capabilities of the Indian armed forces. Further, *the key challenges to Indo-Russian defence cooperation in the context of Indian aspirations and Russian pragmatism will be discussed.* This will follow up with the conclusion.

India-Russia Relations in the Historical Framework

India-Russia relations represent almost a half century of unique, close, cooperative and cordial relations. The foundations to it were laid in 1950s when the then Prime Minister of India, Jawaharlal Nehru visited Soviet Russia in 1955, followed by the Soviet premier's visit in the same year. During his visit, Khrushchev supported India's territorial sovereignty and integrity thereby backing India on Kashmir dispute and on the issue of India's claim for Goa. This backing proved to be of mutual help wherein it represented a successful foray of Soviet Union into Third World country and India's attempt to rise in the global arena. It was followed up with substantial economic and military assistance from the Soviet Union to India during much of 1960s-1970s. Soviet Union gave access and agreed to co-produce with India its one of the most cutting edge fighter aircraft, MIG 21. This was exceptional on the ground that Soviet Russia denied this technology to China. This also served India to counter balance itself with regard to the Chinese threat. Soviet Union thus remained neutral during the Sino-India border dispute of 1962.

After the Indo-Pak War of 1965, Soviet Union provided platform for peace negotiations between the two countries. Soviet Union again helped India during the 1971 War with Pakistan. The Soviet conduct and generous help in 1965 and 1971 reaffirmed India's faith in the friendship with Soviet Union as a dependent ally. This closeness continued to expand by the subsequent governments in India throughout the 1980s.

The major change of the trajectory in the India-Soviet Russia relations came after the end of Cold War and subsequent disintegration of the Soviet Union. The successor state Russia found itself in a completely different situation—its power reduced, and its once robust military industrial technologies became a major economic burden for the new state. Domestically in India too, economic liberalization replaced the earlier protectionist policy. India became a good market for foreign investments.

In the defence parlance, the dependence on Soviet Russia received a jolt after its disintegration; and thereby India started diversifying its defence requirements on a wider scale. The global intense Cold War era rivalry was replaced by new global call for war on terrorism. The changed international dynamics brought India-U.S. close to receiving a new boost to their otherwise thorny relations of the past. All these factors presented a new challenge to the India-Russia exceptional friendship.

The new leadership in both the countries was pragmatic to realize that they need to re-adjust and re-orient their relations to sail in future. This was followed by creating new avenues of co-production, and research and development over buyer-seller relations in the defence sector. India-Russia have also expanded their political relations from mere backers to movers in various international and regional forums—UN, BRICS, SCO, North-South Corridor, Afghanistan are some of the examples. This was largely made possible by the signing of The Declaration of Strategic Partnership in 2000. India-Russia relations have also diversified from the Cold War period of defence to other sectors too viz. space, energy, science and technology, cultural, nuclear deal etc.

As detailed by ex-Indian Foreign Secretary Rajan Mathai, the five major components of India-Russia partnership include politics, defence, civil nuclear energy, anti-terrorism cooperation and space with the economic relations being given a new impetus in recent years (Sharma, 2012). The official statements and policy framework documents too refer to the importance accorded to their bilateral relations. Relations with Russia are a key pillar of India's foreign policy and Russia has been a long standing time-tested partner of India (MEA, 2014).

India-Russia Defence Cooperation

India-Russia defence cooperation remains one of the important foundations of their bilateral relations. Russia continued to be the main supplier of arms for Indian armed forces. Up to 70 percent of Indian military hardware owes its origin to Russia (Report, 2004). Over the years, defence relations between India and Russia have evolved from a simple buyer-seller relationship to a broad-based partnership wherein both the countries are involved in joint designs and development and production of defence equipment (Ministry of Defense, 2009). Despite the recent trends of Indian diversification of its arms procurement, Russia still receives a big share of Indian defence purchases.

India-Russia relations developed in the period of intense Cold War rivalry. USSR was highly instrumental in strengthening of the Indian armed forces. Their cooperation is exceptional and cannot be defined in simple terms of bilateral relations. Soviet Russia stood by the side of India during the Indo-Pak War, and stayed neutral during Indo-China War. It sold defence hardware which it even denied to communist China, thereby placing India at par in the USSR political establishment (Donaldson, 1972). In the post-Cold War era, their cooperation transformed from strategic partnership to strategic cooperation. It has supported India's stand on Kashmir and they find many common grounds in international politics despite sharing no close proximity.

Three important landmark agreements between the two countries cemented their present strong and exceptional defence relations on a firm footing. First, the "*Indo-Soviet Treaty of Friendship 1971*", ensured supply of huge military aid by the Soviet Union. This treaty checked China and U.S. in tilting towards Pakistan during the conflict. India drew closer to USSR, and started depending on Soviet arms. USSR generously supported India through military and economic aids which were denied by other Western nations. After the disintegration of the USSR, this special relation was inherited by Russia which continued despite the changed circumstances. Russia remained the only country which has transferred key strategic technologies to India (Purshottam, 2011-12).

The second landmark agreement was the *"Treaty of Friendship and Cooperation 1993",* signed after the disintegration of the USSR, which led to a smooth transition of their relationship. It resolved the long pending issue of debt repayment between the two, normalized their ties and tilted Russia's balance in South Asia towards India (Yadav, 2005). The third agreement was *"The Declaration on Strategic Partnership 2000*", (Lavrov, 2007), signed during President Putin's visit to India. This formal 'strategic partnership' agreement between the two nations took India-Russia ties to new heights. It formulated the ties in acquiring a qualitatively new character with enhanced levels of cooperation in almost all areas of bilateral relationship including defence (Sharma,

2012). This agreement concluded defence deals worth US$ 3 billion (IDSA, 2000). The deal also upgraded the IRIGC Military-Technical Co-operation from the level of defence secretaries to the level of Defence Minister on Indian side and the Deputy Prime Minister in charge of defence export on the Russian side (Bakshi, 2006).

For the supply of weapons especially after 1990s, India and Russia signed numerous MoUs during the visits of Primakov (1998), Putin (2000), Vajpayee (2001), George Fernandes (2003), Putin (2014) etc. for building long-term strategic partnership (Yadav, 2005). Bilateral projects currently underway include indigenous production of T-90 tanks and Su-30-MKI aircraft, supply of MiG-29-K aircraft and Kamov-31 and Mi-17 helicopters, upgrade of MiG-29 aircraft and supply of Multi-Barrel Rocket Launcher Smerch. Production of the Brahmos cruise missile could be cited as a successful example of co-production. The two countries are also engaged in joint design and development of the fifth generation Fighter Aircraft and Multi-Role Transport Aircraft (Embassy of India, 2014).

Thus, some of the key features of this exceptional India-Russia Defence Cooperation include: (a) supply of arms to India, (b) technical assistance, (c) joint production, and (d) institutional mechanism for defence deals.

Mechanism of Defence Cooperation

The India-Russia Inter-Governmental Commission is the main driving force for cooperation between the two nations. It is the most comprehensive agreement which India have with any country in the world. Analysts believe it to be the main steering committee that takes their bilateral relations forward in a sustained manner (Sharma, 2012). Under this umbrella, the IRIGC on Military-Technical Cooperation (IRIGC-MTC) was setup in 2000 and is valid till 2020. Under its aegis, the two defence ministers meet annually, alternately in Russia and India, to discuss and review the status of ongoing projects and other issues of military technical cooperation. There are two

Working Groups and seven Sub-Groups under the IRIGC-MTC, which review and discuss an array of military technical issues. In 2008, a high level committee called the High Level Monitoring Committee (HLMC) was set up with Defence Secretary from the Ministry of Defence of the Republic of India and Director of Federal Service for Military Technical Cooperation (FSMTC) from the Russian Federation as its co-chairs (Embassy of India, 2014).

IRIGC-MTC enshrines the interest of the two governments to further develop and strengthen the military and technical cooperation in the sphere of research and development, production and after sales support of armament systems and various military equipments (Embassy of India, 2014). Russia is the only country with which India has an institutionalized annual defence cooperation mechanism at the level of the Defence Ministers of the two countries (Defense, 2013-14). The two sides also have periodic exchanges of armed forces personnel and military exercises. Joint Army and Navy exercises between the two armed forces are held under the title INDRA (Embassy of India, 2014).

Indian Defence Forces: An Overview

India has the third largest armed forces in the world and is making serious efforts to improve their capabilities through arms procurement, joint exercises and indigenous development of military technologies since 1990s. With around 14 percent, India is one of the largest importers of global arms trade (SIPRI, 2014) and is expected to purchase more than US$ 35 billion worth of arms purchases in the near future. This has been the result of several overlapping domestic and international factors.

The restructuring of the Indian economy in 1990s provided India with resources to devote sufficient money for defence requirements. Indian defence budget grew rapidly for the year 2013-14 and remained at ₹ 2.04 trillion (US$ 3.3 billion) (Balance, 2014). India is among the top 10 defence spending nations of the world and spent US$ 46.1 billion in 2012 alone, which is also 2.8 percent of its GDP (SIPRI, 2014). The total strength of Indian armed forces hovers around 13,25,000 active service personnels with total reserve personnels amounting to 11,55,000 (Balance, 2014). Despite this remarkably huge armed personnel and defence budget, India's own domestic defence-industrial growth rate has been significantly very low. Thereby, India is largely dependent on import of military hardware, making Indian defence market contesting and competitive for the world's top arms exporter powers.

Domestically, India is facing armed insurgency in the region of J&K and North-East and from left-wing Naxal threats. India had suffered and is suffering from terror attacks, resulting in loss of lives and huge economic costs. The threat perceptions today have moved away from conventional to non-conventional threats where terrorism, drug trafficking and organized crimes are major threats. These new challenges have necessitated India to equip its armed forces with cutting edge military hardware to protect its sovereignty. Further, these non-conventional threats cannot be tackled alone and need deeper cooperation with other countries.

Looking at India's own indigenous production, some of the important defence hardware includes Tejas Light Combat Aircraft, Dhruv Light Combat Helicopter, Arjun Main Battle Tank, Missile programmes, INS Arihant, besides several frigates etc. However, its own defence production has remained very slow, with cost overruns and delays. According to analysis undertaken by Institute for Defence Studies and Analyses (IDSA), between 2006-07 and 2010-11, India's defence self-reliance index varied between 36 percent and 48 percent, well below the 70 percent India had planned to achieve by 2005 (Balance, 2014). These have an adverse impact on self-reliance, thereby making India seeking overseas defence acquisition.

In August 2013, the Defence Minister revealed that India's

arms imports amounted to ₹ 495.9 billion (US$ 10 billion) between 2012-13 and 2010-11. This does not include 'indirect' arms imports, such as components and raw materials. Some of the big ticket purchases in pipelines included 125 MMRCA fighter planes, attack helicopters, artillery guns, long range maritime surveillance aircrafts and heavy-lift cargo planes.

Challenges to the Indian Defence Cooperation with Russia

Despite a robust and an exceptional defence relation, there have emerged glitches in their relationship. Several factors could be attributed to it. Their coming together was somewhere influenced by Cold War era politics. The imperatives from Indian side was guided by India-U.S. estrangement, the Sino-Pak strategic relationship and the Sino-Pak-U.S. strategic convergence, while the Russian considerations were Sino-Russian military confrontation, the Sino-U.S. quasi-strategic relationship of the 1975-1980s and the Russian need to reach out to the Third World countries through India (Kapila, 2009). Now both India and Russia no longer share the same dynamics of Cold War era. The present global scenario has made compulsions on both the sides—India and Russia to continue the strategic relationship but in a changed environment, the contours of the relations must also harmonise with India's national interests (Menon, 2008). It has become more pragmatic and practical wherein both weigh their options keeping in mind their national interests.

India's own security environment has dynamically changed. It is now defined by a complex interplay of regional and global imperatives and challenges. The size and the strategic location of the country places it at the centre of a security dynamic, impacted concurrently by the positive forces of regional and global connectivity on the one side and by the consequences arising from unpredictability, instability and volatility in parts of immediate and extended neighbourhood, on the other hand (Defense, 2013-14).

The end of Cold War dealt a blow to the otherwise thriving

Russian defence sector. It lost its Soviet-era market and thus had to compete in the open. The aid to defence sector from the government evaporated. This decelerated the Russian defence industry which no longer produced and matched with the West. Its R&D decreased and much of its hardware and technologies have not been upgraded. Though in comparison with the West, its hardwares are robust but unfortunately, Russian fabrication technologies, quality approaches, and accountability have often been poor. The result? A swath of poorly performing equipment that cannot overcome those deficiencies (Staff, 2008). Russian military capabilities are tuned more in line with conventional war and not with the present era of high velocity short war or more technologically driven war. Russia is left behind West in this race. In order to fill this gap, Russian military technologies thus need investments which can be through the sale of arms at market prices. It has also compelled Russia to diversify its defence exports.

These complexities of Russian defence industry have pushed India to look beyond Russia in its defence purchases. Though the diversification in Indian defence sector is not new but what has changed is the increased competitiveness and decreasing monopoly of Russian military hardwares. India is in need of wide variety of defence platform that suits its expanded defence requirements. Russian defence industry somewhere lacks behind in this regard as compared to the West. Other than that, there has been displeasure shown by the Indian side over cost overruns, delivery delays and substandard quality of spare parts.

Unlike the earlier times, Russia too has now become more practical and is offering defence products at market prices and not on friendly prices to India. It wants to encash the defence deals with commercial benefits. There have been consistent delivery delays from the Russian side, which became the issue of a major disagreement. The transfer and refit of INS Vikramaditya became a major souring point in this regard.

India had to pay US$ 2.33 billion for its refit, instead of the original US$ 974 million earmarked in the January 2004 contract under which the carrier was to be delivered by August, 2008 (Pandit, T.O.I, 2012), but was finally delivered in 2014 (DID, 2015).

In a major shift, Russia has started selling the same military hardwares to China. It was away from the undeclared understanding of past between the two nations where Russia blocked sale of same products to other nations which it sold to India. This helped India maintain an edge in the region. Now, India believes this new shift in Russia is going to pose serious challenges to its security needs in the near future. Russia sold Su-35 to China which in turn reverse engineered it to produce its own variant. This has undermined India's edge over China. Further fear has been shown over the transfer of Russian technologies to Pakistan through China. This will jeopardise Indian preparedness over Pakistan. In a marked departure from the past, Russia has recently agreed to sell military combat helicopters to Pakistan during the first ever visit of its defence minister in 45 years to Pakistan (Sharma, 2014). This was a first of its kind agreement between the two countries and it was described as a 'milestone' in their bilateral relations in Pakistan (Ramachandran, 2014).

This was taken seriously from the Indian defence point of view. However, Russia was quick to add that the sale had nothing to do with India, and the exceptional relations with India are on firm ground. But, this was seen as an early warning to India's growing closeness with the U.S.

Russia too has showed its displeasure with the growing closeness of India with the U.S. The dynamics of India-U.S. relations changed with the end of Cold War. India's foray with economic liberalization opened up the Indian market for U.S. companies. The issue of terrorism that came on world politics centre-stage after 9/11, brought India and the U.S. closer, to counter common threats. U.S. restrictions on India were eased up and arms sales picked up. In a clear departure from the past,

Indo-U.S. Nuclear Deal of 2008 proved to be a turning point. Politically, this was an exceptional deal with regard to transfer of nuclear energy to India. The diplomatic negotiations thus achieved in shedding the suspicion towards each other and also less restrictive transfer of U.S. technologies to India. U.S. soon topped the list of Indian defence purchases with some big ticket deals that included transport aircrafts, long range marine reconnaissance aircraft etc. Over the years, armed forces from both the countries had been regularly taking part in military exercises. This has to an extent questioned the otherwise all-weather friendly Indo-Russian relations.

Conclusion

Over the years, India has transformed from a conventional fighting force to a more active force. India is one of the largest contributors of personnel for UN peacekeeping operations. Its geo-political position makes it sensitive to any developments far beyond its borders. It has carried out successfully, large evacuation of Indians from the war and disturbed zones of Lebanon, Iraq, and Syria in recent times. India has effectively demonstrated its blue water capabilities by conducting anti-piracy operations in Gulf of Aden along with other friendly nations.

In line with India's broadening strategic horizons, its military acquisition is seeing a marked shift from conventional land-based systems to means of power projection such as airborne refuelling systems and long-range missiles. India is setting up bases abroad, patrolling the Indian Ocean to counter piracy and protecting the crucial sea-lanes of communication, and demonstrating a military assertiveness hitherto not associated with it (Giriharadas, 2008). India is now participating in various military, naval and air force exercises with different countries to boost its capability and learning while creating a close co-operation. Some of the significant exercises which have been a regular affair are India-U.S., India-Russia, India-China, India-Australia, and India-U.K.

exercises. This clearly indicates a marked departure of operationality of the Indian defence forces (Ved, 2007).

Apart from the domestic factors, the change in international politics has also compelled India to diversify and modernize its defence forces. The 1990s saw the end of Cold War, wherein India's own policy of NAM became imprudent. India was one of the founding members of the NAM ideology, despite that it maintained a close relation with the USSR which included advanced arms transfer at friendly prices. As a counter to it, U.S. maintained close defence relations with Pakistan. But, the disintegration of USSR changed these dynamics of relations in the region. The ebbing away of the threat from communism and the present problem of global terrorism forced U.S. to now seek greater involvement with India. Also, the break-up of Soviet Union alarmed India for its over dependence on Soviet weapons.

It is in this complex and changed background that India has to pursue its policy towards Russia. The end of ideological confrontation between the U.S. and Russia after the Soviet collapse means that if India leans in favour or against either of the two countries, it is no longer in the context of communism versus democracy or state control versus free enterprise in the economic field. India has every reason to arrange its defence relations with countries in accordance with its own needs and the potential of the individual relationship (Sibbal, 2011). Compared to any other time in its history, India faces an international environment that has so far allowed it to pursue a "multi-vector" defence policy as its relations with all major global powers are on a stable footing (Pant, 2010).

The mechanism and robustness of its relations with Russia provides enough room to address the contentious issues cropping between the two. There is now clearly an understanding between the two nations to address the contentious issue and reorient their bilateral relations to sustain the new challenges. In continuation with this, the bilateral relations have over the years expanded and have incorporated several areas for cooperation and thus developing a 'privileged strategic partnership' (Kumar, 2016).

At the same time, India-U.S. defence cooperation will take years to reach up to the level of India-Russia cooperation. India's defence cooperation with Russia is institutionalized along with regular military exercises, while with the U.S., it is more on joint military exercises and some smart big ticket defence purchases. The idea of joint production with the U.S. will take time because of the U.S. behaviour of bullying and halting defence deals. Thus, it will continue on the present level of continued military exercises and buying of some advanced military hardwares. Defence relations with both the countries are augmented on two different parameters. Hence, it is a misnomer to believe that India will jump to the U.S. kitty in the near future. The new international security scenario and global defence industry has now provided India with other options too to buy its weapons than only with Russia or the U.S.

Undoubtedly, Russia will remain one of the prominent suppliers of military hardware to Indian armed forces despite certain glitches and diversification. During the concluding visit of the Russian President's to India in 2014, this has been clearly outlined by the Prime Minister of India (Wilson, 2014). India has assured Russia that it will remain India's 'principle partner' in defence sector, as part of its 'Make in India' initiative (Hindu, 2015). The defence relations between the two countries have evolved from 'buyer-seller' to joint production. The Programme for Military Technical Cooperation signed between the two countries and valid up to 2020 enshrines the interest of the two governments to further develop and strengthen the military and technical cooperation in the sphere of research and development, production and after sales support of armament systems and various military equipments (India, 2015).

Hence, we can conclude that India is smartly balancing its defence cooperation with keeping in sight its own defence requirements and strategic compulsions. India's decision of eliminating both Russia and U.S. from the billion dollar MMRCA deal clearly reflects this trend of Indian defence establishment of playing safe and sticking to its original requirements.

References

Bakshi, J. (2006), "India-Russia Defence Co-operation", *Strategic Analysis,* Vol. 30, No. 2, pp. 449-466.

DID (2015), available at: http://www.defenseindustrydaily.com/ins-vikramaditya-may-hit-delay-cost-increases-03283.

Donaldson, R.H. (1972), "India: The Soviet Stake in Stability", *Asian Survey,* Vol. 12, No. 4, p. 475.

Embassy of India (2014), "India-Russia Bilateral Relations", available at: http://www.indianembassy.ru/priorities_political.html.

Giriharadas, A. (2008), "Land of Gandhi Asserts Itself as Global Military Power", New York: New York Times.

IDSA (2000), "Indo-Russian Strategic Partnership for Enhanced Cooperation", *Strategic Digest,* Vol. 30, No. 11, pp. 1154-1156.

Lavrov, S. (2007), "Russia and India: Mutually Beneficial Cooperation and Strategic Partnership", *International Affairs,* Vol. 53, No. 3, pp. 24-29.

Menon, A.M. (2008), "India-Russia Strategic Relations", *Indian Defence Review,* Vol. 23, No. 1, pp. 178-182.

Ministry of Defence (2013-14), "Annual Report", New Delhi: Ministry of Defence, Government of India.

Ministry of External Affairs (2014), "India-Russia Relations", New Delhi: Ministry of External Affairs, Government of India.

Pandit, R. (2012), *Times of India*, January 25, available at: http://timesofindia.indiatimes.com/india/Admiral-Gorshkov-delay-upsets-India/articleshow/16648280.cms.

Pandit, R. (2015), "Cold War Rivals in the Battle to Become New Delhi's Leading Arms Supplier", *Times of India*, p. 12.

Pant, H.V. (2010), "Indian Defense Policy at a Crossroad", *Asia-Pacific Review,* Vol. 17, No. 1, pp. 12-14.

Purshottam, S. (2011), "Indo-Russian Strategic Partnership", SP's Military Year Book, pp. 9-12.

Sharma, R. (2012), "Indo-Russian Inter-Governmental Commission to meet in mid-October", available at: http://in.rbth.com/articles/2012/09/26/indo-russian_inter-governmental_commission_to_meet_in_mid-ctober_17907.html.

Sharma, R. (2012), "Top Indian Diplomat Explains Russia's Importance to India", available at: RBTH:www.in.rbth.com/articles/2012/11/28/top_indian_diplomat_explains_russian_importance_to_india_19391.html.

Sibbal, K. (2011), available at: http://www.vifindia.org/article/2011/june/10/India-relations-with-the-US-and-Russia#sthash.eDwJp0uH.dpuf.

SIPRI (2014), "SIPRI Yearbook", SIPRI.

D.I.S. (2008), available at: http://www.defenseindustrydaily.com/Russias-Military-Spending-Jumping-But-Can-Its-Industry-05087.

Ved, M. (2007), "India Strategic", available at: http://www.indiastrategic.in/topstories45.htm.

Wilson, N. (2014), *International Bussiness Times*, available at: http://www.ibtimes.co.uk/india-russia-renew-vows-over-defence-partnership-1479129.

Yadav, R. (2005), "India-Russia Strategic Partnership: Implications for Common Security of Asia", in M. Singh (ed.), 'Building New Asia', New Delhi: Shipra.

8

China Factor in India's Neighbourhood Policy

Srikanth Thaliyakkattil

The Indian government's invitation to the heads of SAARC countries and the Prime Minister of Mauritius to attend Narendra Modi's swearing in as the India's 15th prime minister was considered as a fresh and proactive move to engage India's neighbourhood. The participation of the leaders, especially the Pakistan Prime Minister Nawaz Sharif was regarded as a diplomatic triumph. Media and policy experts contrasted Modi's neighbourhood diplomatic initiative with the perceived failure of the previous government. From an Indian point of view, it also implicitly emphasized the centrality of India in South Asian affairs. In spite of all the emphasis of new start, innovative diplomacy etc., Modi's emphasis on neighbourhood diplomacy in substance was only a continuation of previous governments' diplomatic initiatives; the only difference is in the form and style.

The initial positive energy created by the Modi government initiatives came down crashing within the first year of the government. This is mainly because India never changed its perception on the basis on which it conducts its neighbourhood diplomacy. The perception of the Indian neighbours towards India and India's perception towards them vary a lot, the lack of empathy from the India's part played an important part in deteriorating the relationship with the neighbours, and the methods the government employed, especially the unofficial blockade of Nepal, [1] soon proved that the Indian government never changed its old methods and policies.

The result of India's lack of ability to think or perceive issues from its neighbour's standpoint led to many frictions between India and other South Asian countries. South Asian countries always wanted an outside power to balance and deter India in South Asia, and China was and is the best fit for that role. Since 1960s, India's actions and perceived proclivities towards hegemony in South Asia acted as a push factor for the neighbouring countries to have more close relations with China; it increased the attractiveness of China as an economic and security partner, as well as a counterweight to India. However, with the rise of China as a super power, its views and roles also changed in South Asia. South Asia became a lower level priority in its foreign policy, but India's views, especially related to strategy and security are still caught up in the Cold War period. This paper argues that the Indian perception of China's increasing influence in its neighbourhood as a factor harming India's interests in the region is not based on facts, and it is largely a misperception.

I. In Search for the Other

All most all of India's South Asian neighbouring countries have their identities defined in relation to India. Their cultural and historical inter-linkages are so great and complex with India, that they find it necessary to defend their uniqueness to carve out a separate identity for themselves. Because of the huge material, economic and other hard power disparities existing between India and its neighbours, Indian attempts to influence and impose its will, which it considers as its national interest, gives rise to nationalist and anti-Indian sentiments in these neighbouring countries.

This is especially true with Nepal, Sri Lanka, Bangladesh, Maldives and Pakistan. In the case of Pakistan, the perceived threat from India is used by the Pakistani military to thrive and legitimize its dominance in the Pakistani society, and the anti-Indian propaganda and anti-Indian terrorist groups supported or otherwise by the Pakistani military establishment sustains and perpetuate a sense of mistrust and fear between India and Pakistan, and Pakistani elites tries to portray themselves as a

West Asian country than a South Asian country to separate its identity from India. [2] In the post-1962 India-China border War scenario, Pakistan found China as a useful hedge against the perceived threat from India, and with the effort of both Pakistan and the Chinese governments over the years, the close relations between Pakistan and China still sustains today.

The thirty year civil war between LTTE (The Liberation Tigers of Tamil Eelam) and Sri Lankan government was the defining period in India-Sri Lanka relations. There was mistrust between Sri Lanka and India during many phases of the civil war. Since in the initial phases of the rebellion, India overtly and covertly supported LTTE, so obviously Sri Lankans rightly blame the Indian establishment for the rise of the LTTE. [3] At the later stages of the LTTE rebellion, India including China, Pakistan, U.S. and many other countries helped Sri Lanka to defeat LTTE, but the post-War Sri Lanka's active engagement with China is considered by Indians as interference in their backyard.

Born out of War between India and Pakistan, Bangladesh also has its identity interlinked to the Indian state of West Bengal, and it fiercely protects its identity and emphasises its uniqueness and independence from the Indian influence. A large section of the Bangladeshi population holds anti-Indian feelings based on perceived and real anti-Bangladeshi actions of India. For instance, Bangladeshis perceive that India controls the flow of river water to Bangladesh to India's advantage, and Bangladesh alleges that their citizens are frequently being killed by the Indian Border Security Force (BSF). Trade imbalance in favour of India and many other issues also led Bangladesh to seek external balancing of India using China. China in various ways fulfils Bangladesh's need for a counter weight against India. [4]

Nepal's culture, society and economy is closely connected to India. A Hindu kingdom initially and later a Federal Democratic Republic, Nepal is the only Hindu majority state among Indian neighbours and arguably closer to the Indian nation. However,

Nepal detested India's interference in its internal matters, and always craved to balance overwhelming Indian influence, and they found in China a natural partner for balancing India. Maldives a small island state, heavily dependent on tourism revenue is also having close cultural, historical and ethnic relations with India, and at the same time, it also experienced Indian intervention in its internal politics. [5] Hence, like other fellow South Asian countries, Maldives also had enough reasons to have close relations with China.

II. Fact of Geography

India's South Asian neighbours find themselves in a unique geographical position, they do not share boundaries with each other but with India, it is a cart wheel like structure and the centre of the wheel is India. Arguably, the immediate South Asian states sharing boundaries with India have a feeling of isolation which added to India's comparative superiority in size, population and hard power making the South Asian neighbours feel more vulnerable in their relationship with India. China also shares many geographical factors which India has in relationship with other South Asian countries. For instance, China shares boundaries with Pakistan (de facto), Bhutan, Nepal, and Afghanistan, which makes it geographically a South Asian country.

However, culturally, China is a foreign country to South Asia, and except with India, China did not have any major military conflict with any other South Asian country. South Asia, unlike in the case of India, is not a region of primary concern for Chinese strategic and foreign policy thinking. The South Asian countries, except India, find it attractive to have close relations with China, it does not have the historical and ethnic religious baggage which most of the South Asian countries have with India. The rise of China as an economic super power and the Security Council membership it has and its role as a military hardware supplier without strings attached, are other factors which attracted South Asian countries stated towards China. For

South Asian countries in India's neighbourhood to strive for and having a close relationship with China is a natural phenomenon. The perceived increasing closeness of South Asian countries towards China caused concerns in the Indian establishment and to compete with this increasing Chinese influence became an overwhelming concern for the Indian governments.

III. Historical Legacy

Nehru never considered the Himalayan states neighbouring India as independent, and on many occasions, he reiterated this belief. According to one of his letter to a political official in Sikkim in 1952 by expressing his concerns over Indian border, he mentions, "we (India) are particularly concerned with our border states like Bhutan, Sikkim and Nepal and in no event will tolerate any intrusion in these states". [6] This shows that the Himalayan kingdom's boundaries are de facto Indian boundaries. India's neighbouring countries always remained the central concern of the Indian diplomacy—for these countries are considered as the immediate buffer zone, any outside powers influence on these countries are considered as negatively influencing the Indian interests.

The Indian foreign policy was initially informed by two contradictory ways of thinking: one is the victim mentality as a victim of colonialism and at the same time to a large extent following the colonial master's strategic thinking in its neighbourhood policy which forms the core of India's external policy. As the victims of colonialism, Indian foreign policy was based on anti-imperialist and anti-colonialist rhetoric, and moral support to the anti-imperialistic and anti-colonial struggles going on during the initial decades of Indian independence.

Indian leadership was largely trained in British educational system and ways. They inherited most of the British institutions after the Independence, which were previously used to exploit and subjugate India; so it was easy for the

Indian leadership to absorb various contradictions such as to follow liberal democracy and other institutions of the British in a illiterate and starving country like India, i.e. giving a premium to the Western liberal values than to economic development and ignoring the fact that West became democratic and liberal after attaining a certain degree of economic prosperity or to put it differently, Western democratic system is built on economic prosperity than the other way round.

India also supported the anti-imperialist struggles of the third world against the Western powers, and followed the same imperialist policies around its neighbourhood. The Indian elites also held an idealized view of communism in the initial period, though this is not true towards the home grown communism in India. This form of thinking led to the emergence of glaring contradictions. For example, India was against imperialism of the West, but was silent towards the communist imperialism and its atrocities. The bias against the West and a pre-disposition towards "peaceful intentions" of the communist countries clouded India's national interest priorities. Another obvious contradiction was adopting the imperial tendencies and the British Indian Empire's strategic thinking in its relation with its smaller neighbours and at the same time advocating non-interference and non-alignment.

The initial foreign policy contradictions are actually the reflections of Nehru's personality. Until his death in 1964, it was Nehru who formulated and directed the foreign policy of India. According to Pinak Ranjan Chakravarty, (a former secretary of the MEA), the personal imprint of Nehru was so overwhelming that he became the sole arbiter of India's external relations. [7] Nehru's foreign policy ideals still influence the foreign policy thinking of India, especially because for a larger period of post-Independent India has been ruled by his descendents, hence they had a vested interest in defending and legitimizing Nehru's foreign policy.

Nehru's views on India's neighbours still have strong

influence on the views of the Indian elites. According to Nehru's assessment of India's security situation in 1950, in spite of India's "desire to settle any points at issue between us and Pakistan, and developing peaceful relation with it, the fact remains that our major possible enemy is Pakistan". Nehru also assumed that if India "falls out completely with China, Pakistan will undoubtedly try to take advantage of this, politically or otherwise". [8] Nehru in his cable to K.M. Panikkar analyzed that in view of the problems persisting in Nepal politics, "there is risk of disgruntled elements in Nepal trying to play India and China off against each other". [9] So in the initial years of India's Independence, Nehru was concerned about the role China may play in South Asia. The current Indian concerns about China more or less correlate with Nehru's concerns. Thus, Indian perception about China's role in its neighbourhood is consistent. However, the question is whether these perceptions are helpful or harmful to Indian interests and whether these perceptions are based on rational thinking and facts.

Sri Lanka in the initial years of its Independence was not so friendly towards China and was apprehensive towards India and according to Nehru, an insignificant country internationally. [10] Accordingly, due to changes in its governments, Sri Lanka's foreign policy flipped between cordial and not so cordial in terms of relations with China. For instance, under the first Sirimavo Bandaranaike government (1960-1965), the Sri Lankan foreign policy became anti-Western and Sri Lankan relations with China reached its peak of cordiality since its Independence, in spite of pressures from public and opposition. Sirimavo Bandaranaike remained neutral during and after the India-China War of 1962, and in a way pro-China. Then in 1963, Sri Lanka signed a Maritime Agreement with China conferring reciprocal most-favoured-nation treatment in relation to the sea-borne traffic.

The next Sri Lankan government led by Senanayake reverted to pro-Western policy. This trend of Sri Lankan foreign policy continues till today with various hues. [11] Nehru treated the Himalayan Border States as pseudo-Indian states, and was not in favour of other countries, especially the big powers establishing relations with these states. Evidently, he vetoed any normal foreign relations of these countries. According to the then Soviet Union president Khrushchev, in the initial years after India's Independence, Soviet Union and China both did not send their ambassadors to Nepal—"the reason was that Nehru did not want Soviet and Chinese ambassadors there". [12] According to the Chinese view, in the 1960s, Nepal is an anti-Indian country, and Nepalese resent the Indian influence. [13] China and Nepal signed the boundary agreement, thus settling the boundary issue between them. In contrast, since 1950s onwards, Nepalese hold varying degrees of anti-Indian sentiment.

IV. Perception and Misperception

Post-1962 India-China war, the legacy of treating and seeing surrounding countries as a buffer zone got only strengthened, and China became the most important "threat" and negative influence India should watch out for in the neighbouring South Asian countries. During the post-Cold War era, increasing economic relations between India and China did not have much of an impact on this perception of India, and for one of the most defining aspects of the post-Cold War period, the rise of internet and social media only helped in strengthening these perceptions and spreading it far and wide. One of the problem which emerged in the internet era is how easily the English media can influence the thinking of the world, especially because the medium of dominant global media is the English language. Indian strategic elites, like any other third world country elites, were and are vulnerable to the influence of Western dominated media and strategic thinking.

One case in point is the widely propagated "string of pearl" strategy of China. The first mention of this strategy can be found in a report titled, "Asia's Energy Security" entrusted by the American Defence Department's, Office of Net

Assessment and written by the Booz Allen Hamilton Company (a strategy and technology consulting company), which was submitted to the then United States Secretary of Defence, Donald Henry Rumsfeld. The report mainly dealt with the series of Chinese strategies for the protection of the important sea lanes. [14] This "string of pearls" construct widely propagated by media and foreign strategic experts also got the attention of the Indian experts and became a "fact" in Indian strategic thinking. According to the Indian version of this strategy, China is surrounding India by constructing naval facilities in its neighbourhood.

Some of the prominent Indian policy and strategic experts who gave credibility to these views included Professor Srikanth Kondapalli. According to him, the fear that China is surrounding India with ports or China's "string of pearls" is not a fear, but a fact. [15] Another prominent strategic thinker Harsh V. Pant believes that by building close relations in India's neighbourhood, China managed to restrict India's manoeuvrability in its own backyard. [16] Extrapolating the "string of pearls strategy", the former Indian Navy chief, Arun Prakash, opined that China has created "weapon-client states" such as Myanmar, Bangladesh, Pakistan, Saudi Arabia and, Iran to surround India. [17]

The threat propagated about China's building of listening stations and other military facilities in Myanmar turned out to be false, especially in relation to the rumoured facilities built by China on Coco Islands of Myanmar close to the Bay of Bengal. [18] Singapore is the largest investor in Myanmar, and China, Thailand and Singapore are the top three largest trading partners of Myanmar, and Myanmar also has close relations with India and of late increasingly getting closer to the United States. China has economic and commercial interests in Myanmar just like any other country, and strategic interests too because Myanmar is China's neighbouring country and has internal ethnic issues, sometimes even spilling over to the Chinese territories. These factors and facts makes China's interests in Myanmar legitimate, thereby establishing its relations with Myanmar as a normal one.

For Bangladesh, investment from any source will be a welcome prospect, and the country needs investment to improve its colonial era infrastructure, especially the port facilities. China has a record of building world class infrastructure in a short period of time. It is quite predictable that Bangladesh also wants to attract Chinese expertise and investment to improve its infrastructure. Bangladesh is also engaging with other countries like India and Japan for the same. Bangladesh has its own various economic and strategic considerations and it engages with various world powers to realize its interests. For instance, Bangladesh had a nuclear deal with Russia, and U.S. and U.K. are the largest aid donors to Bangladesh. So, it is clear that Bangladesh deals with other countries according to its national interests, defined in terms of economic development, and China is one of them.

The following detailed analysis of Indian perceptions on China's relations with the two most important neighbours of India, Sri Lanka and Pakistan, shows that the basis of India's negative perceptions on China's close relations with its neighbours are largely irrational.

Sri Lanka: Indian leaders from the Initial years of Independence itself saw Sri Lanka as a crucial part of India's defence and security strategy. According to the Indian National Congress President in 1949, "India and Ceylon must have a common strategy and common defence strength and common defence resources. It cannot be that Ceylon is in friendship with a group with which India is not in friendship—not that Ceylon has no right to make its own alignments and declare its own affiliations—but if there are two hostile groups in the world, and Ceylon and India are with one or the other of them and not with the same group, it will be a bad day for both". [19] Nehru while pointing out Sri Lanka's close cultural relations with India predicted that Sri Lanka will eventually draw into union with India presumably as an autonomous unit of the Indian Federation. [20] This thinking of the Indian leaders can be also read as the Indian foreign policy framework towards Sri Lanka. The Indian attitude eventually led to active interference in Sri Lankan internal and external affairs.

India, actively involved in the thirty year Sri Lankan civil war between the LTTE and the Sri Lankan government, ended up becoming the enemy of both sides. [21] Many Sri Lankans believe that India is one of the main actors responsible for the destructive civil war, and from time to time when India try to put political pressure on Sri Lanka, it is pointed out by the Sri Lankan politicians. For instance, in 2013, the then Defence Secretary of Sri Lanka, Gotabaya Rajapaksa responded to the Indian pressure by mentioning India's role in destabilizing Sri Lanka. According to him, "had India acted responsibly, Sri Lanka would not have experienced a 30-year war, and India could never absolve itself of the responsibility for creating terrorism in Sri Lanka". [22]

Following Rajiv Gandhi's assassination by the LTTE, India also became hostile towards the LTTE and since the post-September 11 terrorist attacks and subsequent American "war against terror", Sri Lanka got global support to eliminate the LTTE. However, the Western and the Indian support were half-hearted—both advocated that a military solution to the LTTE problem is impossible. However, Sri Lanka pressed with the military solution to completely eliminate LTTE, and had to face Western sanctions for it. The main hope for Sri Lanka was China's support for the Sri Lankan efforts to defeat the LTTE. China actively supported Sri Lanka, or even it can be said that without China's help, Sri Lanka would have never won the war against the LTTE.

When in the name of the Sri Lanka's deteriorating "human rights" record, U.S. ended direct military aid to Sri Lanka in 2007, and Sri Lanka seemed yet again succumbing to the pressures of the West and India, as well as had to take dictation from the West about what is good for Sri Lanka, China came to the help of Sri Lanka, both with financial aid and militarily equipment, increasing aid to nearly US$ 1 billion to become the Island's biggest donor, giving tens of millions of dollars' worth of sophisticated weapons, and making a free gift of six F-7 fighter jets to the Sri Lankan air force. And, crucially, China prevented the UN Security Council from putting Sri Lanka on its agenda. [23]

Since 2009, when the three-decade civil war between Colombo and Tamil separatists ended, Beijing has pumped an estimated US$ 5 billion into Sri Lanka, thus actively participating in the reconstruction of the war ravaged country. [24] This may sound a good thing for a rational person, but India as well as the West were opposed to the increasing Chinese involvement in Sri Lanka, and one of the biggest developmental projects in the Sri Lankan history, the Hambantota Port project became symbolic in raising the fears of India and the West about the "China threat".

Hambantota Port project was initially offered to India, and when bidding for the development of the port was invited in 2005, the Indian companies were not much interested in bidding, doubting the wisdom of investing in a project which may not be commercially viable. [25] In 2007, China won the bid to build the Hambantota Port, but this port project was widely reported in the Western and Indian media and the tone was that it is harmful for the Indian interests in the region. This led to concerns in the Indian diplomatic and strategic circles. Another port project, namely the Colombo Port expansion project, partially funded by the ADB and won by China, is also viewed through the China threat angle, but just like Hambantota, it was also won by the Chinese companies through open bidding. There were no Indian entities participating in the bids, leaving the Chinese consortium as the sole bidder for the terminal. [26] Another project, the "Port City" project which is built on the reclaimed land from the Colombo Port Expansion project and funded and built by the Chinese companies also became the biggest source of worry for India and the West.

Mahinda Rajapaksa, under whose presidency, Sri Lanka won the civil war with LTTE, actively encouraged close economic relations with China, and thus became a target of Western and Indian displeasure. Rajapaksa has visited China seven times during his nine years tenure (2005-2015) in office. Considering that China is the second largest trading partner of Sri Lanka, the largest investor in Sri Lanka and the largest aid donor to Sri Lanka, Sri Lankan president's visits look obvious. The visit of a Chinese submarine to Sri Lanka in 2014 was considered as the breaking point among the relations between the Rajapaksa government and India. However, according to Rajpaksa, it was a normal visit. He also pointed out, "when ever Chinese submarines come to this part of the world (Sri Lanka), they always inform India. The Chinese president was here, so the subs were here. Find out how many Indian submarines and warships came to our waters when the Indian prime minister came for the SAARC Summit in 2008". [27]

However, the perceived closeness of Sri Lankan president towards China is also termed as against the Indian interests. Rajapaksa lost elections conducted in January 2015 and has blamed the U.S. and THE European governments as well as India's secret service for this loss. According to him, "It was very open—the Americans, the Norwegians, and the Europeans were openly working against me as also the RAW (Research and Analysis Wing: the Indian intelligence agency)". [28] Before the election defeat, the Rajapaksa government accused RAW of galvanising support for a joint opposition ticket for Maithripala Sirisena, who later won the elections and became the President of Sri Lanka, after persuading him to split from the Rajapaksa cabinet. The new president Maithripala Sirisena ran for presidency in a covertly anti-China plank. He promised to halt and review the Chinese funded and built port projects, and also vowed to source cheaper loans from elsewhere.

After his victory, his first visit was to India and the Indian Prime Minister Narendra Modi also visited Sri Lanka. Sirisena suspended a Chinese funded US$ 1.4 billion 'port city' project in Colombo that India considered as a security risk, and ordered a review of the other Beijing-financed projects and loans amid allegations of corruption. [29] However, in the post election scenario, the new government soon faced the realities. It has failed in its stated aim of replacing 70 percent of the more than US$ 5 billion that Sri Lanka owes to the Chinese lenders with loans at cheaper interest rates and of longer durations from the other governments. [30] Soon Sri Lanka approved the renewed construction of the China funded "port city" and also other China funded projects. [31]

Sri Lankan prime minister also mentioned that it will continue to have close relations with China, and will also allow the visit of Chinese naval vessels and submarines. [32] This means that Sri Lanka needs China more than China needs Sri Lanka. For instance, nearly seventy percent of the infrastructure projects in the country have been funded by China and built by the Chinese companies. Sri Lanka's relationship with China is helping Sri Lanka to transform itself into a major transhipping hub in Asia, and it is also largely benefiting the Indian companies considering that seventy percent of the transhipment business through Colombo port is Indian. However, the Indian paranoia about "China threat" from Sri Lanka persists. The reflection of this paranoia is that India maintains its four diplomatic missions in Sri Lanka, and one of the missions is in Hambantota and it was inaugurated in 2010, after China got the project to build a port there. [33]

One other factor which proves India's fear about China's role in Sri Lanka is irrational in the sense that Sri Lanka also maintains close relations with the U.S. and other major world powers. In 2007, Sri Lanka and the U.S. signed the "Acquisition and Cross-Servicing Agreement", providing more interoperability between the Sri Lankan military and the American military. [34] U.S. financial institutions are major investors in Sri Lankan bonds, and U.S. is the largest market for Sri Lankan exports, accounting for around 25 percent of its exports. [35] India is the largest trading partner of Sri Lanka and has extensive investment relations with Sri Lanka. So for Sri Lanka, China is equally important just like India or the U.S. and that China is only one of the players in Sri Lanka and Sri Lanka deals with these powers according to its national interests.

Pakistan: China's all-weather friendly relationship with Pakistan is regarded as one of the core concerns of the Indian security establishment. Rationally, China's relation with Pakistan can be considered as a normal relation between any two countries. Pakistan is not overwhelmingly dependent on China for its economic development. For instance, China is only one of the top trading partners of Pakistan—in 2014, the top trading partners of Pakistan were the EU, U.S. and China in the stated order. However, the most important concern of India is China's arms sales to Pakistan as well as the close military cooperation between the two countries. Pakistan's close military relations with China is mainly for the reason that Pakistan is and was more or less forced to buy Chinese weapons because of the on and off sanctions imposed by the U.S. since 1965. Irrespective of the change in the global political environment, China has been a consistent arms supplier to Pakistan. However, Pakistan always sought more sophisticated and advanced weapons from the U.S. and Europe. Chinese weapons were not a favourite but the next best choice for the Pakistani military.

Most of the sophisticated weapons in Pakistan's possession are supplied by the U.S. and European countries. United States in order to protect its perceived national interests was the main supplier of most advanced weapons for the Pakistani military. Chinese arms transfers to Pakistan are well publicized and discussed by the Indian analysts. On the other hand, the U.S. weapons sales and grants to Pakistan are not so publicized. Though this is the case, the breadth and depth of American arms transfers to Pakistan since 2001 is staggering. Most of these transfers are financed by military grants from the

U.S., which means it is mostly free, and given away in the name of counter terrorism. It is worthwhile to quote the entire range of these transfers to understand the decisive role of the U.S. in improving Pakistan's military edge against India.

"The Pentagon reports total foreign military sales agreements with Pakistan worth about US$ 5.4 billion for the period 2002-2014; (sales of F-16 combat aircraft and related equipment accounted for nearly half of this). The Congress has appropriated about US$ 3.6 billion in Foreign Military Financing (FMF) for Pakistan since 2001. These funds are used to purchase U.S. military equipment for long-term modernization efforts. Pakistan also has been granted U.S. defence supplies under the Excess Defence Articles (EDA) (the left over weapons and equipments of Afghan and Iraq war). Cost includes training and support too". [36] Following is a comprehensive list of weapons and equipments supplied by the U.S. to Pakistan since 2001.

Major post-2001 defence supplies provided, or soon to be provided, under the FMF include the following:

1. Eight P-3C Orion maritime patrol aircraft and their refurbishment (valued at US$ 474 million—four delivered, three of which were destroyed in a 2011 attack by the Islamist militants).
2. At least 5,750 military radio sets (US$ 212 million).
3. 2,007 TOW anti-armour missiles (US$ 186 million).
4. Six AN/TPS-77 surveillance radars (US$ 100 million).
5. Six C-130E Hercules transport aircraft and their refurbishment (US$ 76 million).
6. Perry-class missile frigate USS McInerney, via special EDA authorization (US$ 65 million for refurbishment; now the PNS Alamgir).
7. 20 AH-1F Cobra attack helicopters via EDA (US$ 48 million for refurbishment, 12 delivered).
8. 15 Scan Eagle reconnaissance unmanned aerial vehicles (US$ 30 million). [37]

Supplies paid for with a mix of Pakistani national funds

and the FMF include as under:

1. Up to 60 mid-life update kits for F-16A/B combat aircraft (valued at US$ 891 million, with US$ 477 million of this in FMF; Pakistan has purchased 45 such kits, with all upgrades completed till date).
2. 115 M-109 self-propelled howitzers (US$ 87 million, with US$ 53 million in FMF). [38]

Notable items paid or to be paid for entirely with Pakistani national funds include the following:

1. 18 new F-16C/D Block 52 Fighting Falcon combat aircraft (valued at US$ 1.43 billion).
2. F-16 armaments including 500 AMRAAM air-to-air missiles; 1,450 2,000-pound bombs; 500 JDAM Tail Kits for gravity bombs; and 1,600 Enhanced Paveway laser-guided kits, also for gravity bombs (US$ 629 million).
3. 100 Harpoon anti-ship missiles (US$ 298 million).
4. 500 Sidewinder air-to-air missiles (US$ 95 million).
5. Seven Phalanx Close-In Weapons System naval guns (US$ 80 million). [39]

Major articles transferred via EDA include the following:

1. 14 F-16A/B Fighting Falcon combat aircraft.
2. 59 T-37 Tweet military trainer jets.
3. 374 M113 armoured personnel carriers. [40]

"Under the Coalition Support Funds (in the Pentagon budget), Pakistan received 26 Bell 412EP utility helicopters, along with related parts and maintenance, valued at US$ 235 million. Under Section 1206 of the Frontier Corps and Pakistan Counterinsurgency Fund authorities, the United States has provided 4 Mi-17 multirole helicopters, 4 King Air 350 surveillance aircrafts, 450 vehicles for the Frontier Corps, 20 Buffalo explosives detection and disposal vehicles, helicopter spare parts, explosives detectors, night vision devices, radios, body armour, helmets, first aid kits, litters, and other individual soldier equipment. Through International Military Education and Training and other programs, the United States has funded and provided training for more than

2,000 Pakistani military officers.

In April 2015, the State Department approved a possible US$ 952 million FMS deal with Pakistan for 15 AH-1Z Viper attack helicopters and 1,000 Hellfire II missiles, along with helicopter engines, avionics, training, and support". [41]

China is only one of the countries which helped Pakistan to attain its nuclear capabilities; financial support of oil rich Arab countries, complacency of the European countries and the U.S. also played a big part. [42] If we apply the same logic that India applies to depict Chinese threat in our neighbourhood, then U.S., EU and the GCC states are all threats to India. Pakistan's inimical intentions towards India is a standalone one, and China is not a factor in that, but definitely Pakistan uses whatever tool it has; in some cases it is China, to maintain a perceived balance of power in South Asia.

V. Conclusion

China is the largest trading nation in the world. It is the largest trading partner of more than 124 countries (comparable statistics for India is 2-6 countries depending on the year). So obviously, China also has close trade relations with the South Asian countries which is quite normal. China is also one of the largest investor in the world—so it is natural to invest in South Asian countries too. China's largest investment destination is the U.S. and the EU countries therefore, its investment in South Asia is not unique. Unlike the U.S. and the EU countries, China provides cheap and affordable defence equipment without much "strings attached". Hence, Chinese weapons are popular with the third world countries which also hold true to India's neighbouring countries.

India's source of misperception is its own weakness and reliance on foreign sources to know about China. Over the years, India neglected its own economy and defence sectors. Therefore, comparing with China make India's look weaker. For instance, China's nominal GDP is more than five times that of India and the defence budget is around four times than

India's. China has a huge indigenous defence capability, and India still relies on different countries for its defence needs. From time to time, the memories of the 1962 War whipped out by the media and experts, also led India to attribute negative intentions on China's every move in its neighbourhood and take actions accordingly, which from the perspective of neighbouring countries is interfering in their internal affairs and blocking the development initiatives and economic growth of these countries.

Ironically, India itself has close economic interaction with China and actively courts Chinese investments. India also is not a role model for economic development or internal stability, so most of the South Asian neighbours may not want to pursue the Indian economic model. India holds top position in some of the worst indicators of poverty, malnutrition and economic development. So one can assume that none of India's neighbours want to be like India in economic terms, and China provides an attractive alternative. One of another important factor is that our neighbouring countries are all sovereign countries and they engage with almost all major powers of the world, economically and strategically to realize their national interests. Considering South Asian countries' huge hard power disparity with India and geographical proximity, hypothetically it will be suicidal for them, except in the case of Pakistan, to court active inimical relations with India.

So India should embrace the economic engagement of China in South Asia and actively encourage Chinese enmeshment in South Asia. It will provide rich dividends to South Asia as well as China, and create stake holders in all sides who have interest in maintaining a stable South Asian region. On security and strategy front, only India's internal economic development and defence modernization can provide India with a long-term sustained security.

Endnotes

1. Dixit, Kunda, "India and Nepal Have No Choice but to End

Their Border Dispute and Move On", *Time*, November 17, 2015, available at:
http://time.com/4115801/nepal-india-border-blockade-madhesh. Ojha, Hemant, "The India-Nepal Crisis: After Two Devastating Earthquakes: A Blockade on its Border Presents Nepal with Another Humanitarian Crisis", *The Diplomat*, November 27, 2015, available at:
http://thediplomat.com/2015/11/the-india-nepal-crisis.

2. Zaidai, S. Akbar (2009), "South Asia? West Asia? Pakistan: Location, Identity", *Economic and Political Weekly*, Vol. XILV, No. 10, pp. 36-39.
3. Srinivasan, Meera, "India Responsible for 30-year War: Gotabaya Rajapaksa", *The Hindu*, April 11, 2013, available at: http://www.thehindu.com/news/international/south-asia/india-responsible-for-30year-war-gotabaya-rajapaksa/article4605639.ece.
4. De Silva, K.M. (1995), "Regional Powers and Small State Security: India and Sri Lanka, 1977-1990", The Johns Hopkins University Press, pp. 304-305; Anam, Tahmima, "How Bangladeshis See India", *The Guardian*, August 14, 2007, available at:
http://www.theguardian.com/world/2007/aug/14/india.features115; Sengupta, Ramananda, "Why Bangladesh Hates India", *Rediff*, December 22, 2005, available at:
http://www.rediff.com/news/2005/dec/21bspec.htm.
5. Brewster, David, "Operation Cactus: India's 1988 Intervention in the Maldives", *Pragati*, April 18, 2014, available at: http://pragati.nationalinterest.in/2014/04/operation-cactus-indias-1988-intervention-in-the-maldives.
6. Nehru, J. (1996), "Selected Works of Jawaharlal Nehru", Vol. 19, second series, New Delhi: Jawaharlal Nehru Memorial Fund, p. 652.
7. Chakravarty, Pinak Ranjan (2014), "India's Foreign Policy in the Neighbourhood", *Indian Foreign Affairs Journal*, Vol. 9, No. 2, p. 138.
8. Nehru, J. (1993), "Selected Works of Jawaharlal Nehru", Vol.15, second Series, New Delhi: Jawaharlal Nehru Memorial Fund, pp. 344-345.
9. Nehru, J. (1993), "Selected Works of Jawaharlal Nehru", Vol. 15, second series, New Delhi: Jawaharlal Nehru Memorial Fund,

p. 643.

10. Nehru, J. (1999), "Selected Works of Jawaharlal Nehru", Vol. 25, second series, New Delhi: Jawaharlal Nehru Memorial Fund, p. 376.
11. De Silva, K.M. (1981), "A History of Sri Lanka", Los Angeles: University of California Press, p. 532.
12. Record of Conversation of N.S. Khrushchev with CCP Chairman Mao Zedong, Deputy Chairman Liu Shaoqi, Zhou Enlai, Zhu De, Lin Biao, Politburo Members Peng Zhen and Chen Yi, and Secretariat Member Wang Jiaxiang, October 2, 1959, History and Public Policy Program Digital Archive, APRF, copy on Reel 17, Volkogonov Collection, Library of Congress, Washington DC. Translated by David Wolff.
13. Fifth Official Meeting Between the Delegation of the Albanian Labour Party and the Delegation of the Chinese Communist Party, June 19, 1962, History and Public Policy Program Digital Archive, Central State Archive, Tirana, AQPPSH-MPKK-V. 1962, L. 14, D. 6. Obtained by Ana Lalaj and translated by Enkel Daljani.
14. Qing, Liu (2010), "String of Pearls Strategy: India's Perception and Responses", *South Asia Quarterly*, Vol. 141, No. 2, p. 22.
15. Devichand, Mukul, "Chittagong One of China's Pearls?", *BBC*, May 17, 2010, available at: http://news.bbc.co.uk/2 /hi/business/8687917.stm.
16. Pant, Harsh V. (2010), "China's Naval Expansion in the Indian Ocean and India-China Rivalry", Vol. 8, Issue 8, No. 4, available at: http://www.japanfocus.org/-Harsh_V_-Pant/3353.
17. Cherian, John, "The Battle is On", *Frontline*, Vol. 24, Issue 18, September 8-21, 2007 available at: http://www.hinduonnet.com/fline/fl2418/stories/20070921508013100.htm.
18. See Egreteau, Renaud (2008), "India and China Vying for Influence in Burma: A New Assessment", *India Review*, Vol. 7, No. 1, pp. 38-72.
19. Kodikara, Shelton U. (1982), "Foreign Policy of Sri Lanka: A Third World Perspective", New Delhi: Chanakya Publications, p. 23.
20. Wriggins, William Howard (1960), "Ceylon: Dilemmas of a New Nation", New Jersey: Princeton University Press, p. 399.

21. Mishra, Akshaya, "Indira Gandhi Helped Train Tamil Rebels, and Reaped Whirlwind", *First Post*, May 23, 2011, available at: http://www.firstpost.com/world/indira-gandhi-helped-train-tamil-rebels-and-reaped-whirlwind-13913.html.
22. Srinivasan, Meera, "India Responsible for 30-year War: Gotabaya Rajapaksa", *The Hindu*, April 11, 2013, available at: http://www.thehindu.com/news/international/south-asia/india-responsible-for-30year-war-gotabaya-rajapaksa/article4605639.ece.
23. Popham, Peter, "How Beijing Won Sri Lanka's Civil War", *The Independent*, May 23, 2010, available at: http://www.independent.co.uk/news/world/asia/how-beijing-won-sri-lankas-civil-war-1980492.html#gallery.
24. Patranobis, Sutirtho, "Chinese Influence Wanes on Sri Lanka's Shifting Sands", *Hindustan Times*, September 9, 2015, available at: http://www.hindustantimes.com/analysis/chinese-influence-wanes-on-sri-lanka-s-shifting-sands/story-G6t9dPhfnNt0aUte3oaFNK.html.
25. "India Refused to Build Hambantota Port: Rajapaksa", *Rediff*, March 18, 2010, available at: http://www.rediff.com/news/report/what-mahinda-rajapaksa-says-about-indo-lanka-ties/20100318.htm;
Anand, Vinod, "Strategic Connotations: Development of Hambantota Port", *Vivekananda International Foundation*, February 29, 2012, available at: http://www.vifindia.org/article/2012/february/29/strategic-connotations-development-of-hambantota-port.
26. Bagchi, Indrani, "China to Build Another Port in Sri Lanka", *Times of India*, September 17, 2010, available at: http://timesofindia.indiatimes.com/india/China-to-build-another-port-in-Sri-Lanka/articleshow /6567958.cms.
27. Chowdhury, Debasish Roy, "Sri Lanka Should Thank China, Not Attack It, Ex-president Rajapaksa Says", *South China Morning Post*, March 12, 2015, available at: http://www.scmp.com/news/asia/diplomacy/article/1735379/sri-lanka-should-thank-china-not-attack-it-ex-president.
28. Press Trust of India, "As Modi Visits Sri Lanka, Rajapaksa Blames India for his Election Defeat", *Indian Express*, March 13, 2015, available at:

http://indianexpress.com/article/world/neighbours/as-modi-visits-sri-lanka-rajapaksa-blames-india-for-his-election-defeat.

29. AFP, "Sri Lanka's New Leader Heads to China After Winding Back Ties", *Daily Mail*, March 23, 2015, available at: http://www.dailymail.co.uk/wires/afp/article-3007166/Sri-Lankas-new-leader-heads-China-winding-ties.html.
30. "All Chinese Infrastructure Projects to Proceed: Sri Lanka Says", *VOA*, December 17, 2015, available at: http://www.voanews.com/content/all-chinese-infrastructure-projects-proceed-sri-lanka/3107722.html.
31. Peiris, Vilani, "Sri Lankan Government Lifts Suspension on China-funded Port City Project", *World Socialist*, December 28, 2015, available at: https://www.wsws.org/en/articles/2015/12/28/sril-d28.html. Popham, Peter, "Sri Lanka is Welcoming China and its Money Once More", *Independent*, December 11, 2015, available at: http://www.independent.co.uk/voices/sri-lanka-is-welcoming-china-and-its-money-once-more-a6770201.html.
32. Velloor, Ravi, "Sri Lanka to Allow Chinese Submarines to Visit, says PM Wickremesinghe", *The Straits Times*, October 18, 2015, available at: http://www.straitstimes.com/asia/south-asia/sri-lanka-to-allow-chinese-submarines-to-visit-says-pm-wickremesinghe.
33. Anand, Vinod, "Strategic Connotations: Development of Hambantota Port", *Vivekananda International Foundation*, February 29, 2012, available at: http://www.vifindia.org/article/2012/february/29/strategic-connotations-development-of-hambantota-port.
34. Reddy, B. Muralidhar, "U.S-Sri Lanka Sign Logistics Pact", *The Hindu*, March 6, 2007, available at: http://www.thehindu.com/todays-paper/tp-international/us-sri-lanka-sign-logistics-pact/article1806378.ece.
35. Pennington, Matthew, "The US Wants to Lure a Strategic South Asian Island Nation Away from China", *Business Insider*, February 2, 2015, available at: http://www.businessinsider.com/the-us-wants-to-lure-a-strategic-south-asian-island-nation-away-from-china-2015-2?IR=T.
36. Congressional Research Service, "Major U.S. Arms Sales and Grants to Pakistan since 2001", May 4, 2015, available at:

https://www.fas.org/sgp/crs/row/pakarms.pdf.

37. Ibid.
38. Ibid.
39. Ibid.
40. Ibid.
41. Ibid.
42. See Levy, Adrian and Catherine Scott-Clark (2007), "Deception: Pakistan, The United States and The Secret Trade-in Nuclear Weapons", New York: Walker.

9

India and Tibetan Autonomy: A National Security Perspective

Rakhee Viswambharan

India inherited the British policy of keeping Tibet as a buffer zone. In the post communist revolution, India urged China to maintain Tibet's autonomous status, as it suites India's security interest to minimize China's military presence in the region. However, the invasion of Tibet by People Liberation Army of China in 1951 put an end to Tibet's status as a buffer zone. It exposed the Indo-China border as undefined and invalidated the agreement between Tibet and British India on border delineation. In 1951, Tibet was forced to sign a 17 point agreement with China and Tibet become part of People's Republic of China. Though, China termed its invasion of Tibet as 'peaceful liberation', gross human rights violations had taken place in Tibet. By the end of 1950s, Tibetans rose in an attempt to independence known as the 'National Uprising'. The Tibetan system of government was replaced and Dalai Lama and his followers were forced to seek asylum in India. The Tibetans in India formed a government in exile at Dharamsala. India's decision to provide asylum to Dalai Lama and his followers was one of the irritant in Indo-China relations.

Ultimately, it resulted in the Indo-China war of 1962 and China had annexed a large part of strategically important territory of India. Tibetans are distinct people with their own language and culture. They also form a large majority of the population of Tibet. The UN General Assembly passed a resolution in 1959 in support of the right to self-determination of the people of Tibet.

The disintegration of Soviet Union and the formation of a large number of new nation states in Eastern Europe on the basis of right to self-determination of the people once again brought the Tibetan issue before the international and regional organizations. As a major stake holder in the Tibetan issue, India's stand assumes great significance. Further, if the Tibetan struggle for self-determination eventually results in Tibet's autonomous status, it very well serves India's security interest to minimize China's military presence in the region.

Autonomy versus Self-determination

Generally, the right to self-determination is the right of people to determine their own destiny. In particular, the right allows 'people' to choose their own political status and to determine their own form of economic, cultural and social development, free of outside interference. Exercise of this right can result in a variety of different outcomes ranging from political independence to forms of autonomy or association to full integration within a state. The importance lies in the right of choice, so that the outcome of people's choice should not affect the existence of the right to make a choice. In practice, the possible outcome of an exercise of self-determination will often determine the attitude of governments towards the actual claim by people.

Thus, while claims to cultural autonomy may be more readily recognized by states, claims to independence are more likely to be rejected by them. Nevertheless, the right to self-determination is recognised in international law as a right of process, and not of outcome, belonging to people and not to states or governments. It is important to note that self-determination has never simply meant absolute independence. Most importantly, it is meant as the free choice of people to determine their status. This right remains an ongoing choice of the people as to their governance, and their economic, social and cultural development. It is a constant entitlement. It must also be emphasised that democracy in itself does not necessarily satisfies the requirements for the implementation of self-determination although democracy and aspects of self-determination are closely linked. In cases where democracy is defined as the rule of the majority and the people claiming the right to self-determination constitutes a numerical minority in the state in question, a democratic system does not necessarily respond to the needs of the minority people. [1]

UN and Right to Self-determination

After the Second World War, the principle of self-determination was developed in various UN instruments. The United Nations Charter Article 1(2) states: "The purposes of the United Nations are to develop friendly relations among nations based on the respect of the principle of equal rights and the self-determination of peoples...Again Article 55 enjoins each member state of the United Nations to create stability and well-being "based on respect for the principle of equal rights and self-determination of peoples". [2] The UN Charter was followed by the Universal Declaration of Human Rights (UDHR) of 1948. [3] Again, by 1960, with the adoption of the Declaration on the Granting of Independence to Colonial Peoples, the principle was elevated to the position of an unconditional right. [4]

This declaration and the related declaration, the Declaration Concerning the Implementation of the Right to Self-determination, affirmed the right to immediate self-determination for peoples under "alien, colonial or oppressive domination" and called for a "speedy and unconditional end to colonialism in all its manifestations". [5] The Declaration on the Granting of Independence marks a significant shift in the law of self-determination. For the first time, in the case of colonial entities, it stressed that "inadequacy of political, economic, social or educational preparedness should never serve as a pretext for delaying independence". [6] Meanwhile, the Declaration Concerning the Implementation of the Right to Self-determination outlined three methods by which the self-determination of non-self-governing territories could be achieved. These methods are independence, free association and integration, and the standards of democratic participation. The General Assembly had made it clear that the favoured outcome for a process of decolonization was to be independence.

In 1966, the International Covenants on Civil and Political Rights and the International Covenant on Economic, Social and Cultural Rights were adopted and opened for signature, ratification and accession. Article 1 of the International Covenant on Civil and Political Rights states: "all peoples have the rights to self-determination. By virtue of this right, they may freely determine their political status". Article 1(2) of the Covenant notes that self-determination shall include a right to dispose of wealth and resources—economic self-determination, while Article 1(3) obliges state parties to the Covenants "to promote the realisation of the right to self-determination". [7] The ICCPR has been ratified by 161 of the 193 members of the UN. Five other countries including China have signed but not ratified. A nation which is a signatory of an international treaty such as ICCPR is obliged under international law to refrain from acts which would defeat the purpose and objects of the treaty. All nations are therefore bound both by its adherence to UN Charter and by its signature of the ICCPR in respect of the principles of self-determination of the people.

The International Covenants do not appear to limit the right to self-determination to people classified as non self-governing by the United Nations. The implication is that the right belongs to 'all people' and must be respected by all states, not only those who may be in a trust relationship with dependent people. State practice has commonly accepted the legal interpretation that the right to self-determination belongs primarily to people under colonial or alien rule. The applicability of the principles to classic colonial cases was largely unquestioned in the post-World War II period. And nearly a billion people were liberated from colonial rule through its implementation during this period in the Afro-Asian region. The controversy arises particularly when applying to people other than those in classical colonial situations.

The 1971 UN Declaration on the Principles of International Law Concerning Friendly Relations and Cooperation among States, develops the rights of equal rights and self-determination still further and offers alternatives to independent statehood including self-determination through free association with an independent state. [8] Though it declares the rights of all people to have these rights to freely determine, the Declaration sheds little lights as to how the objectives should be accomplished.

Again, the description of the 'people' that comes under the right to self-determination was controversial. In 1989, UNESCO convened a meeting of jurists and scholars to clarify the concept of 'people' rights. In its final report and recommendations, the panel adopted the following description of 'people': (i) A group of individual human beings who enjoy some or all of the following common features: (a) a common historical tradition; (b) racial or ethnic identity; (c) cultural homogeneity; (d) linguistic unity; (e) religious or ideological affinity; (f) territorial connection; (g) common economic life. (ii) The group must be of a certain number which need not be large...but which must be more than a mere association of individuals within a State; (iii) the group as a whole must have the will to be identified as a people or the consciousness of being a people. (iv) The group must have institutions or other means of expressing its common characteristics and will for identity. [9]

If we apply this definition, it appears that, the Tibetan people fulfil all the requirements envisaged in the report. The UN, through various instruments, holds that the right of self-determination is a prerequisite to the enjoyment of all other fundamental human rights.

Again in 1993, the United Nations World Conference on Human Rights held in Vienna, affirmed in the final Declaration which has been adopted unanimously by all states that the right to self-determination is part of the international law of human rights. The declaration states, "All peoples have the right of self-determination. By virtue of that right, they freely determine their political status, and freely pursue their economic, social and cultural development. Taking into account the particular situation of peoples under colonial or other forms of alien domination or foreign occupation, the World Conference on Human Rights recognises the right of peoples to take any legitimate action, in accordance with the Charter of the United Nations, to realise their inalienable right to self-determination.

The World Conference on Human Rights considers the denial of the right to self-determination as a violation of human rights and underlines the importance of the effective realisation of this right. In accordance with the Declaration on Principles of International Law concerning Friendly Relations and Co-operation Among States in accordance with the Charter of the United Nations, this shall not be construed as authorizing or encouraging any action which would dismember or impair, totally or in part, the territorial integrity or political unity of sovereign and independent states conducting themselves in compliance with the principle of equal rights and self-determination and thus possessed of a government representing the whole people belonging to the territory without distinction of any kind". [10]

Tibetan Views on Right to Self-determination

Tibet was an independent, sovereign nation when the PLA of the People's Republic of China (PRC) entered Tibet in 1950. Tibet at that time possessed all the attributes of a state hood. Tibetans argue that even the PRC does not dispute that the Tibetans are a distinct people who in 1950 occupied a distinct territory. Tibet also had a fully functioning government headed by the Dalai Lama and that government, was free from outside interference, administered the welfare of the Tibetan people through civil service, judicial and taxation systems, as well as through a postal and telegraph service, and a separate currency. The government controlled the borders and issued passports to its people, which were recognized internationally. It entered into treaties as a sovereign with other states, including Britain, Nepal and Mongolia. Tibet also negotiated as an equal sovereign with China and Britain at the Shimla Conference of 1914. [11]

With regard to the basic document regarding the annexation of Tibet, the Seventeen Point Agreement of 1951, which China claims resolved Tibet's status, according to Tibetan view point is not a legally binding agreement. The Agreement was signed when PLA occupied large parts of Tibet, and it was signed under threat of further military action in Tibet. A treaty concluded under such circumstances is not legally valid. [12]

Tibetans further argue that once a state exists, it is legally presumed to continue as an independent state unless proved otherwise. The historical evidence not only fails to prove otherwise, but affirmatively demonstrates that Tibet has always been an independent state, despite periods during which it was influenced to varying degrees by foreign powers. [13] They also maintain that even if Tibet had not been an independent nation in 1950, the Tibetan people would nonetheless be entitled to exercise their right of self-determination. International law recognizes the right of the people to self-determination; that is, the right freely to determine, without external interference, their political status and to pursue their economic, social and cultural development. The Tibetans are unquestionably a 'people' and are eligible to claim the right to self-determination. They are entitled to choose independence from China, autonomy with China, or any other political status. [14]

The Tibetans are entitled to exercise their right of self-determination as against the China's claim of right to territorial integrity because Beijing has not acted as the legitimate government of the Tibetan people. A government's legitimacy derives from a people's exercise of the right of self-determination and from its conduct in accordance with its obligation to protect and promote the fundamental human rights of its entire people, without discrimination. The Chinese government in Tibet was imposed on the Tibetans by force, and not by an exercise of self-determination. Moreover, China has persistently and systematically abused the human rights of Tibetans through repression of religion, population transfer, birth control policies, discrimination, and destruction of the environment, involuntary disappearances, arbitrary arrest, torture and arbitrary executions. Therefore, PRC is not the legitimate government of the Tibetan people and it has no claim of the right to territorial integrity to assert against the Tibetan's right to self-determination. [15]

The Tibetans further maintain that a balancing of the fundamental values of the international community also weighs heavily in favour of enforcing the Tibetan's right to self-determination. A non-militarized independent Tibet would enhance peace and security in the region by serving as a buffer zone between the two most populous nations in the world, India and China. The Tibetan's exercise of self-determination will not only promote the international values of respect for human rights and fundamental freedoms but also international peace. Thus, the Tibetans plea for self-determination is mainly based on historical, legal and human rights factors.

Tibetan Struggle for Autonomy

The Tibetan issue is embedded in the history of Tibetan nationalism and Tibet-China relations. The history of Tibetan nationalism and the Tibet-China relations may be divided into four main periods (Smith, 1996; Goldstein, 1989; Grunfeld, 1987). The first phase (630-842) is that of the consolidation of the Tibetan state from the beginning of Tibetan history up to the fall of the Tibetan empire in 842.

Tibet was not again politically unified until the mid-13th century when Tibetan Lamas established a political-spiritual relationship known as 'cho-yon' or 'priest-patron' relationship with the Mongol empire. Tibet was a dependent state under the Mongol Yuan (1260-1368) and Manchu Ching (1644-1911) dynasties. Tibet was independent of Chinese influence during the native Chinese Ming dynasty (1368-1644). During the second phase, Tibet was under the direct rule of China for a short span of three years from 1911-14.

In the third phase (1914-50), Tibet experienced modern imperialist pressures and Tibetan nationalism aroused. Tibetan nationalism was stimulated in the early 20th century by the British imperialist interests in Tibet and Chinese attempt to impose more direct control over Tibet. With the British patronage, Tibet managed to achieve de facto independence, however, it failed to gain international recognition of its independence.

In the fourth period (1950 to the present), Tibetan independence was forcibly eliminated. The People's Liberation Army (PLA) marched into Tibet in the 1950 and annexed Tibet through a 'peaceful liberation'. Under the pretext of peaceful liberation, China had generally imposed its will on the Tibetan people. Tibet was forced to sign an agreement with China in 1951 known as the '17-Point Agreement on Measures for the Peaceful Liberation of Tibet'. The Chinese consider this agreement as a measure to liberate Tibetan territory from imperialist forces. However, it is well known that when the PLA marched into Tibet there were no imperialist forces present in Tibet.

Therefore, from the Tibetan perspective, such 'peaceful liberation' was imposed and promises of autonomy stated in the agreement were not being followed by the Chinese. And the Tibetan national identity comes under intense pressure from China for the 'socialist transformation' of Tibetan society. The Tibetan culture was subjected to assimilationist pressure during the Cultural Revolution (1966-76). However, the Tibetan nationalism survived and grew under the Chinese rule. After 1980, in the period of liberalized Chinese policies in Tibet, Tibetan culture and nationalism revived. During this phase, Tibetans gained international support to their plea for right to self-determination (Smith, 1996).

The great power game was well visible in Tibet from the beginning of the 20th century. In 1904, the British troops entered Tibet and forced it to sign an agreement. This move on the part of Britain was mainly based on the then Viceroy Lord Curzon's perception regarding the Russian moves in Central Asia and in particular the Russian interaction with Tibet. However, the British government in London did not approve the invasion of Tibet and the Chinese suzerainty was once again brought into force. The 1907 convention by Russia China and British India approved the Chinese suzerainty over Tibet.

However, the fall of Manchu dynasty in 1913 once again had given Tibet the de jure independent status. In the 1914 Shimla Convention, Tibet attended along with British India and China (Tibetan Centre for Human Rights and Democracy, Human Rights Situation in Tibet, Annual Report, 2009). The final outcome of the convention was the McMahon line which demarcates the border between British India and Tibet. There is difference of opinion regarding the Chinese approval to the final outcome. However, given the weak power position of China at that time, it had only limited option but to accept the Shimla Convention of 1914. Thus, in the Shimla Convention of 1914, the Tibetan plenipotentiary attended it along with China and British India and this clearly shows that Tibet enjoyed independent status to negotiate with others. This status of Tibet continued till the entry of People's Liberation Army (PLA) in 1950-51 and its annexation of Tibet.

It is important to note that though Tibet was never formally recognized by the League of Nations or the United Nations, Tibet during the period 1913-51 had an independent government, currency, army, judicial and postal systems, and administration. Furthermore, the Tibetan government enjoyed formal bilateral relations with the neighbouring countries of

Mongolia, Nepal, India, and Bhutan, and concluded treaties with China and Britain. The Tibetans claim that they have every right to self-determination as China had illegally occupied their territory in the name of 'peaceful liberation of Tibet' in 1951. The China's annexation of Tibet in fact once again altered the geo-strategic position in the Himalayan region and also nullified the outcome of the Shimla Convention of 1914. It is interesting to examine how Tibetan issue forms a significant factor in India-China relations.

Tibet and India-China Relations

It appears that there are four major issues which form Tibet as a factor in India-China relations. They are as under:

- The position of Tibet.
- Tibetan refugees in India.
- The India-China border dispute.
- Common security concerns.

The Position of Tibet: India's position on the status of Tibet has changed from the British policy of recognising the de facto independence of Tibet—completely Autonomous State—under ambiguous form of Chinese suzerainty to Tibet as 'autonomous region of China'.

Independent India was not very sympathetic to the Tibetan demand for independence. However, when the PLA entered into Tibet, India did not hesitate to deplore China's invasion of Tibet (Mehrotra, 2000:14). In a note dated October 26, 1950, the Ministry of External Affairs, Government of India, told the Chinese foreign office how it looked at the event:

"In the context of world events, invasion by Chinese troops of Tibet cannot but be regarded as deplorable and in the considered judgment of the Government of India, not in the interest of China or peace". This statement clearly shows India's stand on the Tibetan issue in the initial period. [16]

Again, when the PLA entered into Tibet, the Indian Prime Minister, Jawaharlal Nehru stated in the Indian Parliament on December 7, 1950:

"It is not right for any country to talk about its sovereignty or suzerainty over an area outside its own immediate range. That is to say, since Tibet is not the same as China, it should ultimately be the wishes of the people of Tibet that should prevail and not any legal or constitutional arguments—the last voice in regard to Tibet should be the voice of the people of Tibet and of nobody else". [17]

Jawaharlal Nehru's statement in the Indian Parliament was significant in many respects. It reflected India's stand on right of the people. It also manifests a clear understanding of the Tibetan question.

In the beginning, India had supported Tibet's claim for self-determination. However, a marked change in India's stand on self-determination was visible after the Indo-China bilateral agreement of 1954, known as the 'Panchsheel'. [18] As per the agreement, India had accepted China's claim on Tibet. Thus, on April 29, 1954, India relented to the Chinese insistence on referring to Tibet as 'Tibet Region of China'. Though India failed to provide any support to the Tibetans right to self-determination when it was taken up at the UN General Assembly in 1958, India had provided political asylum to Dalai Lama and his followers in 1959.

After the 1962 border War, India often merely used 'Tibet' until the 1988 visit of the then Indian Prime Minister, Rajiv Gandhi when the 'Sino-Indian Joint Press Communiqué' referred to Tibet as 'an autonomous region of China'. Again in 2003, Prime Minister Atal Bihari Vajpayee signed a declaration which recognised 'that the Tibet Autonomous Region is part of the territory of the People's Republic of China' (Declaration on Principles for Relations and Comprehensive Cooperation between the People's Republic of China and the Republic of India, 25 June 2003). However, India's acceptance of Tibet as a part of China is conditional upon Tibet's enjoyment of autonomy. China, therefore, demands stronger and more unambiguous statements from New Delhi on China's sovereignty over Tibet, which India has resisted so far.

Tibetan Refugees in India: India's consistent official Tibetan policy has been to disallow anti-Chinese activities by Tibetan refugees on Indian soil. However, India has allowed the Tibetans to run a government-in-exile, the Central Tibetan Administration. India refuses to bend to Chinese pressure by reducing or suspending its support to Tibetan exiles in India. India will and should continue to support Tibetan refugees because it is in India's national interest. For the foreseeable future, India's material assistance and facilitating role for the Tibetan struggle will continue. This is one of the major irritants in India-China relations. The Chinese complain that such an open encouragement and support given by the Government of India to the Tibetan in their 'anti-China activities' constitute interference in China's internal affairs and obstruct the progress of India-China relations. It appears that India's gravest threat to China lies in Tibet because of the political asylum that India had provided to over 80,000 Tibetans in India. So long as the exiled community exists, Tibetan nationalism and the demand for self-determination will remain a major apprehension for the communist China (Suresh, R., 2011: 246).

India-China Border Dispute: The border dispute continues to avoid a resolution ever since India and China have acquired a common border when the PRC occupied the Tibet in 1951. The historical roots of the Sino-Indian border dispute can be traced to the imperial period during the great game between British India, Czarist Russia and Qing China over Tibet and Central Asia. Empires thrived on uncertain borders—frontiers were more preferable to imperial powers—as clearly demarcated borders constrained their own ambitions and strategic flexibility. In addition, the inhospitable terrain of the high Himalayas, the absence of sophisticated surveying technologies and existence of a functioning Tibetan state made the delimitation of India's northern border either unnecessary or difficult.

Nevertheless, ultimately the Shimla Convention of 1914, in fact, made the border line between British India and Tibet. However, in the mid-20th century, when two equally nationalistic and territorial states gained control over the Indian and Chinese empires, China was not ready to accept the British proposed McMahon line. This stand of China was well reflected especially after the signing of the 'India-China Agreement on Trade and Intercourse between Tibet Region of China and India' (April 29, 1954) in which India for the first time accepted Tibet as a part of China. On the Indian side, Prime Minister Jawaharlal Nehru at the time of signing of the Panchasheel agreement thought that the boundary was no longer an issue, and that the China had accepted the historical status quo.

Jawaharlal Nehru wrote about this to the Chinese Premier, Zhou Enlai in 1958 as the border issue heated up: "When the Sino-Indian Agreement in regard to the Tibet region of China was concluded, various outstanding problems, including some relating to our border trade, were considered...No border questions were raised at that time and we were under the impression that there were no border disputes between our respective countries. In fact we thought that the Sino-Indian Agreement, which was happily concluded in 1954, had settled all outstanding problems between our countries". [19]

He had also expressed shock at seeing maps printed in China showing certain 'Indian' areas to be parts of China.

The India-China border problem is embedded on Tibet as China had no border with India except through Tibet and India's border with Tibet was a well-settled border negotiated at the Shimla Conference of 1914. [20] Thus, it appears that a solution to the Indo-China border problem lays in the implementation of the Tibetan claim for the right to self-determination and the restoration of Tibet's historical status as a buffer zone between India and China.

Further, it appears the communist regime in China is also not very serious about finding an amicable settlement of the border problem due to two important reasons. Firstly, the prevalence of successful democratic system in India poses a challenge to the communist system in China. Any close cooperation and interaction with democratic India would be detrimental to the continuance of the totalitarian system in China. Secondly, the present communist regime in China wanted to keep the border problem unresolved so that they can divert the attention of its own population from the serious domestic issues and also a rationale for its huge defence spending and heavy force deployment along Tibet.

Security Concerns: It appears that Tibet is an important factor in security paradigm of both India and China. Since its geopolitical position has wedged it between two great powers, it has to be dependent on either China or India, having no other choice. Tibet has always had a high degree of spiritual identification with India. The Republican Chinese officials way back in 1910 expressed similar assessments when they stated: "Tibet is a buttress on our national frontiers—the hand, as it were, which protects the face—and its prosperity or otherwise is of the most vital importance to China".

India has its reciprocal fears arising from Chinese military presence in the Tibetan plateau. The true extent of China's military presence in Tibet cannot be gauged, given the extreme secrecy surrounding information about the Peoples Liberation Army. The presence of Chinese strategic forces on the Tibetan plateau adds another dimension to India's China threat perception. Again, India's security perceptions also centred on China's management of water resources originating from Tibet, which in fact feed the Indian subcontinent. The historical memory about betrayal and humiliation on account of the 1962 War continues to casts a shadow over India's perceptions of China.

In essence, the complex of security concerns connected to Tibet underpins the strategic rivalry between the two major Asian players—India and China. Consequently, China and India have common security concerns that are connected to Tibet. These issues can be well addressed only through mutual trust and confidence building measures. Though efforts were made to resolve the border dispute amicably since 1988 through the joint working group (JWG), little progress has been reported so far. Meanwhile, the external powers exploit the conflicting situation to their advantage through various overt and covert moves.

Conclusion

Tibetans are distinct people with their own language and culture. They also form a large majority of the population of Tibet. The UN General Assembly passed a resolution in 1959 in support of the right to self-determination of the people of Tibet. The disintegration of Soviet Union and the formation of a large number of new nation states in Eastern Europe on the basis of right to self-determination of the people once again brought the Tibetan issue before the international and regional organizations. As a major stake holder in the Tibetan issue, India's stand assumes great significance. Further, if the Tibetan struggle for self-determination eventually results in Tibet's autonomous status, it very well serves India's security interest to minimize China's military presence in the region.

Endnotes

1. UN Charter, www.un.org/en/documents/charter.
2. Text of the UDHR, see "Year Book of the United Nations", United Nations Publications, New York, 2006.
3. UNDoc.Res.1541(XV), available at: www.un.org/Depts/dpi/declaration/decolonisation.htm.
4. Ibid.
5. Ibid.
6. Text of the International Covenant on Civil Political Rights. Year Book of the United Nations, United Nations Publication, New York, 2006, available at: www.ohchr.org/english/law/ccpr.htm.
7. UN Declaration on Principles of International Law Concerning Friendly Relations and Cooperation Among States, October 24, 1970, Res. 2625(XXV).
8. See International Meeting of Experts on further study of the

concept of the peoples. Final Report and Recommendations, UNESCO, November 27-30, 1989, Paris.
9. UN Doc. A/CONF.157/23.
10. "Human Rights Situation in Tibet: Annual Report 2009", Tibetan Centre for Human Rights and Democracy, Dharamsala, 2009. See the official web site of Tibetan Government in exile www.tibet.com; also see the UN Doc. A/PV/1394, December 14, 1965, GAOR.
11. Ibid.
12. Ibid.
13. Ibid.
14. Ibid.
15. Ibid.
16. Quoted in L.L Mehrotra, "India's Tibet Policy: An Appraisal and Options", Tibetan Parliamentary and Policy Research Centre, New Delhi, 2000.
17. Ibid., p. 14.
18. (i) Mutual respect for each other's territorial integrity and sovereignty; (ii) mutual non-aggression; (iii) mutual non-interference in each other's internal affairs; (iv) equality and mutual benefit; and (v) peaceful co-existence.
19. Notes, Memoranda and letters Exchanged and Agreements signed between The Governments of India and China White Paper III, MEA, Government of India, New Delhi.
20. Indian Parliament on Issue of Tibet, Lok Sabha Debates, 1952-2005, Tibetan Parliamentary and Policy Research Centre, New Delhi, 2006.

References

Goldstein, Melwyn C. (1989), "A History of Modern Tibet: 1913-1951", Munishiram Manoharlal Publishers Pvt. Ltd., Delhi.

Grunfeld, A. Tom (1987), "The Making of Modern Tibet", Oxford University Press, Delhi.

Lama, Dalai (1988), "Five Point Peace Plan for Tibet", Information Office, Central Tibetan Secretariat, Dharamsala (H.P.), India.

Mehrotra, L.L. (2000), "India's Tibet Policy: An Appraisal and Options", Tibetan Parliamentary and Policy Research Centre, New Delhi.

Smith Jr., Warren W. (1996), "Tibetan Nation: A History of Tibetan Nationalism and Sino-Tibetan Relations", Westview Press,

Oxford.

Suresh, R. (2011), "Tibetan Right to Self-determination and Sino-Indian Relations", *International Journal of South Asian Studies*, Vol. 4, No. 2.

Tibetan Centre for Human Rights and Democracy (2009), "Human Rights Situation in Tibet", Annual Report 2009, Dharamsala, Himachal Pradesh.

UN Doc. A/CONF.157/23.

Zhao, Suisheng (1996), "The Implication of Demilitarization of Tibet for Sino-Indian Relations and Asian Security", *Asian Affairs*, Vol. 22, No. 4, Winter.

10

India's Maritime Challenges in the South China Sea

C. Vinodan

For the first time after 360 years in modern history, the focus of international politics is shifting towards the Asian region and the major Asian powers China and India are simultaneously emerging as new players in global politics. The rise of Asia is arguably one of the most significant developments in international relations in the twenty-first century. These global power shifts manifest one of the most important transformations in international politics in modern history (Bergsten et al., 2006: 1). India and China had already shown their interest in transforming the global power structure through their recent foreign policy initiatives. Both nations are actively engaging with other emerging powers for revamping the global governance architecture. Both possess massive manpower, scientific, industrial and technological bases as well as large armed forces. They are both nuclear powers and have nascent space programmes.

Historically, China and India have demonstrated the capacity and will to act as hegemons, dominating the security environment of their regions (Pant, 2009). They also have a history of rivalry. This manifested itself in the 20th century as War in 1962, as well as armed skirmishes in 1967 and 1987. China's extraordinary growth and active diplomacy has already created a renewed debate among scholars and practitioners regarding the nature of the evolving international system, and it is predicted that future decades will see even greater increases in Chinese power and influence (Ikenberry,

2008).

The question is whether the "great transformation" will be a peaceful process through soft diplomacy and soft balancing or an influential and assertive China seeking to transform international relations to fit its strategic ambitions. The South China Sea symbolises rising China's larger strategic dilemma in the emerging global security order. The South China Sea (SCS) disputes are regarded as one of the most difficult regional conflicts in the Asia Pacific, in an 'arena of escalating contention' (Shen, 2013). Indeed, some scholars suggest that for the next 20 years, the South China Sea conflict will probably remain the 'worst case' threat to peace and security in the Asian region (Acharya, 2013).

Territorial sovereignty, contentions over energy, the significance of the geographic location, the threat to maritime security and overlapping maritime claims are all sources of the SCS disputes. For China, the South China Sea dispute represents the kind of challenge that could determine whether or how China will indeed ascend to superpower status. Regrettably, China does not yet recognize the extent to which its aggressive course in the South China Sea is damaging its diplomacy with the neighbouring countries. [1] This paper reviews the strategic and security challenges manifested in the South China Sea disputes. It also projects the potential areas of conflict among major players in the South China Sea disputes, and the differing perceptions of the major stakeholders in the disputes. The paper also examines the broader strategic significance of the region and the implications of the South China Sea disputes in India's strategic and security planning.

Geo-strategic Dimensions of the South China Sea Disputes.

The South China Sea is a strategic waterway providing the key maritime link between the Indian Ocean and East Asia. The South China Sea is also a large space linking southern China and Taiwan to peninsular and archipelagic Southeast Asia and peninsular and continental Southeast Asia to archipelagic Southeast Asia. The strategic geography of the South China Sea invited more specific challenges, including the potential for conflict between regional states over territory or marine resources and the possibility of conflict between major powers. At the highest level of the threat spectrum, the possibility of conflict between major powers is also rarely absent from such an important sea area, which involves some of the world's busiest and most important sea lines of communication (SLOC). The political sensitivities involved in Southeast Asia, where national interests often clash, or at least diverge, as much as they are shared, make the achievement of a "stable maritime regime", extremely unlikely. [2]

It is in the South China Sea that the components of Asia's changing power dynamics are most concentrated and on display: China's growing strategic heft and paranoid sense of entitlement; its Southeast Asian neighbour's hopes and misgivings about China's regional dominance; and the United States' compulsion to meet China's strategic challenge. The impasse over territorial sovereignty and control of natural resources in the South China Sea represents an increasingly serious challenge to regional security (Clayton, 2012). The South China Sea territorial dispute increasingly looks like a point of strategic friction between the United States and China.

The U.S. Department of State criticized China for its plan to base a new military garrison in the Paracel Islands, saying this would increase international tensions. Beijing shot back that the United States should mind its own business. Many observers wonder why Washington and Beijing are allowing a new irritant to emerge in the incalculably important U.S.-China relationship. U.S. officials have named several specific U.S. concerns about China's policies and activities in the South China Sea, the U.S. concern most widely understood and repeated is the potential threat to "freedom of navigation": the PRC might be moving toward imposing restrictions on foreign ships sailing in the South China Sea (Roy, 2012). The situation demonstrates the need for a more effective and transparent regional security mechanism than currently exists.

The South China Sea is categorized as semi-enclosed sea under the United Nations Convention on the Law of the Sea (the LOS Convention). [3] The South China Sea contains several groups of small islands, rocks and reefs and is claimed by China, Taiwan, Vietnam, the Philippines, Malaysia and Brunei. As to the first facet of the dispute—contested sovereignty claims to rocks and islands—all claimants except Brunei have occupied islands or rocks and have built structures on them. In addition, the South China Sea is the main artery for significant maritime shipping. The main East Asian economic power houses—China, Japan and South Korea—are heavily dependent on the safety and security of the South China Sea lanes. By establishing its static military presence on the Paracel group of islands, China wishes to reinforce its claims and ensure that the others are ousted from the region.

The area bounded by the Sea is approximately three and a half square kilometres and forms a part of the Pacific Ocean. The area includes more than 200 small islands, rocks and reefs with many of them located in the Paracel and Spratly Islands. 33 percent of the world's trade and 50 percent of world's traffic in oil and gas pass through the South China Sea. By establishing sovereignty over rocks and islands, states can claim territorial seas and Exclusive Economic Zones (EEZ) from the islands. These claims bring with them the political imperative to rhetorically defend these claims as part of a state's national identity.

The Philippines, Vietnam and China have all witnessed expressions of grassroots nationalism associated with the islands in the South China Sea, which in some cases has tied the hands of policymakers. Simultaneously, this nationalism discourages cooperation and has served as a legitimizing tool for leaders in all the three states.

The importance of the South China Sea, which borders eight nations—China, Vietnam, Taiwan, Malaysia, Brunei, Indonesia, and the Philippines—has grown as the trade that passes through the area has become integral to the global economy (Bateman and Emmers, 2012). The merchant vessels sailing the waters form a 'super waterway' that connects the busiest shipping ports in the world—Shanghai, Singapore, Hong Kong, Guangzhou—to all corners of the globe. Almost half—in terms of tonnage—of all commercial goods pass through the South China Sea, including over US$ 1.2 trillion in U.S. trade each year. [4] The South China Sea also constitutes a vital section of the seaborne trade route linking both Europe and the Middle East to Northeast Asia; Southeast Asia to Northeast Asia; and much of Southeast Asia to the Pacific Ocean and North America. [5] Its complexity ensures both physical dangers for the safety of navigation and political dangers as a source of international dispute.

A leading factor in the South China Sea has been the disputes over the territorial features and, as a consequence, the potential maritime jurisdiction to which such features may be entitled, including the related living and non-living marine resources. Questions exist over the extent of possible hydrocarbon resources in the central South China Sea. Another factor often overlooked in South China Sea diplomatic discussions is the South China Sea's importance as a fishing ground, accounting for 10 percent of the global catch (Schofield, 2009), with the annual harvest of around 5 million tonnes, representing the fourth largest of the world's 19 major fishing areas. [6]

The South China Sea provides the habitat and spawning grounds for the world's most valuable fisheries of shrimp and tuna, among others (Rosenberg, 2010). Over 500 million people live within a hundred miles, off the shores of the South China Sea and the importance of the fishing industry that feeds and employs this population cannot be overstated (Emmers, 2010). In fact, the political tensions in the South China Sea are more often about fishing rights than military manoeuvres or oil drilling operations. However, the latter are more likely to spark international skirmishes and possibly war. However, at the heart of South China Sea maritime boundary disputes are not today's economic activities like fishing, but the promise of tomorrow's resources. The petroleum passing through the strait, the life blood of all nations, is the major source of oil for Japan, South Korea, and the growing economies of Singapore, Indonesia, Malaysia, and the Philippines. Estimates of oil reserves vary.

The Chinese government estimates that the South China Sea sits upon nearly 200 billion barrels of oil and 266 trillion cubic feet of natural gas (Daly, 2012). The U.S. Geological Survey's conservative projections estimate far less: 4.8 billion barrels of oil and 64 trillion cubic feet of natural gas. It should be kept in mind that the smaller, conservative estimate is still equivalent to Alaska's discovered oil reserves, and more than the discovered gas reserves under the Gulf of Mexico (Hargreaves, 2012). Survey data is scarce due to the Chinese government's efforts to prevent governments and corporations from conducting survey operations in the South China Sea. Even without solid evidence, several oil corporations (e.g., Exxon Mobil, Shell, and Chevron) have expressed interests in making major investments in oil exploration efforts.

The South China Sea, on the western edge of the Pacific Ocean, is vast, over 1.4 million square miles (3.6 million sq. km.) but the two major island groups (Spratly and Paracel) that cover less than six square miles (15.5 sq. km.) are the centre of many disputes. Yet, China, Brunei, Malaysia, the Philippines, Vietnam, and Taiwan have been positioning themselves to claim control over the islands, reefs, and in many cases, some protruding rocks, so as to claim sovereignty, which gives them underground excavation and fishing rights. This has resulted in disputed maritime claims that have existed in the South China Sea for almost a generation. However, the current global recession and a growing demand for oil and natural gas have caused some players to become more aggressive. According to the Southeast Asia Program at the Centre for Strategic and International Studies, twenty-three confrontations have occurred in the region over the last three years.

Major Powers and South China Sea Dispute

The South China Sea dispute is once again under the international security discourse. The tension over sovereignty, resources, and navigation in the South China Sea, and the growing rivalry over primacy in East Asia and the larger Asia-Pacific region, have led to a renewed space for great power rivalry in world politics. At the centre of the disputes are the hardening positions of a number of claimant states. At the same time, there is growing tension between a rising China, poised to exercise greater influence in the region, and the United States as the 'status quo' power determined to preserve its presence in a region of growing strategic salience. Simply put, the South China Sea is becoming a potential flash-point, both because of the unresolved territorial disputes among claimant states, and also as a result of pending great-power rivalry between the United States and China.

The centrality of China's role as a claimant state, and the linkages between its interests in the South China Sea and the development of Chinese maritime power and its overall ambitions for regional hegemony, make the disputes important beyond the limited face value of a few small, scattered islands, rocks, and reefs—or even potential energy resources. China has long been wary of the strategic presence of opposing hegemonic powers in Southeast Asia, who might exploit Chinese weaknesses at sea to apply pressure on China from its southern maritime periphery. China's strategic ambitions in the South China Sea therefore involve the extension of its defensive perimeter, countering the presence of other major powers, countering threats to its territorial and maritime interests by other claimants, and, ultimately, seeking some measure of maritime command over the area to enforce its hegemonic pretensions.

Furthermore, China also has an interest in being able to exert control over East Asian sea lanes, both to safeguard its own oil supplies and to threaten the economic lifelines of Taiwan and Japan if necessary. A permanent strategic presence in the South China Sea, particularly if it can successfully enforce its territorial claims, might conceivably provide China with such ability in the future. The establishment of bases, staging, and surveillance posts along the vital sea lanes has been described as China's "string of pearls" strategy. [7] China has over a period of more than three decades slowly built up its military facilities throughout the South China Sea, including in the Spratlys. In recent years, it has significantly enhanced bases, in particular, on Hainan Island and in the Paraçel archipelago. There have also been reports that the People's Liberation Army (PLA) navy intends to bolster its forces in the area, with a senior PLA officer suggesting that the security situation was "very grim", requiring China to deploy more ships in the disputed region, and to enhance the militarization of occupied features in the Spratlys, including constructing a port for naval vessels and an airport on Mischief Reef, a Chinese occupied reef that lies inside the EEZ claimed by the Philippines (Hsiao, 2009).

Chinese strategists also noted the geopolitical importance of controlling Taiwan and the Taiwanese-occupied islands in the Spratlys if China is to establish a dominating position into the "southern most reaches of the South China Sea". Another driver of naval modernization is the likelihood that these factors have led to a degree of hedging by the Southeast Asian littoral states against strategic uncertainty or the possibility of a significant conflict. Although rarely stated by the regional states, it is fair to suggest that the most likely contingencies that might directly affect the South China Sea area involve China. The possibilities include a conflict over Taiwan, with Japan or the United States, Chinese moves in the Spratlys or against Vietnam, or the external consequences of internal instability within China itself.

Although less likely to lead to armed conflict, the region is also rife with long standing local rivalries. [8] Naval modernization in the South China Sea states thus cannot be attributed to any single factor. While each individual state may have its own priorities, all of the issues discussed above influence most of the littoral states of the South China Sea to a greater or lesser extent. However, the fluid state of great power relations and the rise of China should not be discounted as a leading driver of at least some of the higher end war fighting capabilities being procured, such as the submarines.

Recent upsurge in tensions in the South China Sea represents a security flashpoint with global consequences. The South China Sea is a strategic maritime link and a vital gateway for shipping in East Asia. While it is economically and strategically an integrated entity and a key region for the emerging economies of the Asia-Pacific, many countries have staked a sovereign claim over its waters and islands. The dispute has the potential to turn into a military conflict that could end up affecting thc peace and security of the entire region (Amit Singh, 2011). Naval strategists see China as hemmed in along its sea coast by a chain of states or territories hostile to Beijing: Japan, Korea, the Ryuku Islands, Taiwan, and the Philippines. The overriding goal of Chinese naval strategy is to establish dominance over the waters within this 'first island chain'. [9]

China is both a coastal state with an extensive coastline and EEZ resource claims as well as a user state with a large shipping fleet and a growing dependence on energy imports. [10] China considers that any interruption of tanker traffic through the South China Sea would have immediate negative effects on China's industrial, urban, and transport sectors. The economic dimension of China's maritime security interests, including in the South China Sea, is underscored by the fact that 90 percent of its foreign trade is seaborne (Sakhuja, 2001). The South China Sea also presents a potential opportunity for China to use its territorial claims to gain control of oil/natural gas reserves to deny access to or disrupt supplies. The region contains the heavily disputed Paracel and Spratly Islands with overlapping claims to various areas and energy exploration blocks by China, Taiwan, the Philippines, Vietnam, Indonesia, Malaysia, Brunei, and Thailand. [11]

Over the last 20 years, there have been at least 10 documented disputes over energy exploration rights and 17 military confrontations in the South China Sea and its territories. [12] Some confrontations have resulted in deaths while most have merely jeopardized attempts to exploit energy resources, most significantly between China, Vietnam, and the Philippines. Ultimately, China's extensive claims raise US suspicions over its intent to potentially control the South China Sea and its resources. Such suspicions have evoked strong criticism from the U.S. and other international players which espouses "to intercede to ensure safe passage through international waters" as prescribed by the 1982 United Nations Convention for the Law of the Sea (UNCLOS). [13]

China's disputes with some ASEAN neighbours have severely weakened China's standing in the region and beyond. China's current assertiveness in the South China Sea is now slowly but surely eroding its positive image with its ASEAN neighbours as a peacefully rising power. Without exception, countries within Southeast Asia and beyond are very cautious of China's rise. Even as China's national economic and global stature increase, its influence, image and "soft power" abroad is declining dramatically. China's aggressiveness has resulted in the United States reprioritizing its global strategy with its "pivot" or "rebalance" toward the Asia-Pacific region.

This policy adjustment by the United States has given Chinese policymakers serious reason for concern and activated the fear that China might again end up being contained in much the same way as the former Soviet Union during the Cold War. China now sees "US hands" in both its internal and external affairs. Throughout the region, U.S. allies including Japan, South Korea and the Philippines have all upgraded their already strong military co-operation with the United States. [14]

If China continues to ignore the interests or concerns of its neighbours who have a stake in the South China Sea, its aggressiveness is likely to galvanize increased regional cooperation with the United States. Troubles with close neighbours also affect the image and position of China in the world. The most important condition for any country aspiring to ascend to global power status is to maintain good relations with its neighbours. However, if China is unable or unwilling to maintain a cordial relationship with its closest neighbours, how can countries further afield trust and respect this aspiring superpower? As long as China is unable to maintain a significant level of trust and friendship with its neighbours, benevolent global power status for China is likely to remain a pipe dream. China's dramatic assertion of unilateral sovereignty over the South China Sea has adversely affected the peaceful environment China desperately needs to become a global power. If conflict does break out, it is likely to have a sustained, widespread and long-term detrimental impact on the regional economic and security situation in the region.

US-China Divide

The South China Sea disputes goes beyond the dimensions of sovereignty dispute over energy and resource security. It is being integrated into the field of China's strategic rivalry with the United States as China and the U.S. develop an extended naval strategy and deploys new naval capabilities. Chinese naval strategy has been many years in the making since Chief of the Navy Liu Huaqing (1982-1988) first called for an ocean-going navy to protect China's maritime interests. Over the past two decades, China has been steadily developing naval power, which it has regarded as a necessary attribute of great power status. As China rises in economic power, its maritime interests similarly expand (and with it its naval power), bringing it into conflict with the dominant naval power in the Western Pacific—the United States (Buszyinski, 2012).

The United States has developed unprecedented strategic

interest in the South China Sea dispute in the context of the rapidly changing global political and security order. [15] The U.S. strategic planners consider that a stronger China is challenging important aspects of the long-established Pax Americana, including the U.S. interests across the globe, the U.S. alliance system, and the American involvement in regional issues. A struggle for regional leadership between China and the United States is slowly emerging in different parts of the globe. This is particularly visible in both parties claim in the South China Sea dispute.

Throughout 2010 and into 2011, disputes in the South China Sea were at the forefront of regional tensions involving China, the United States, and the neighbouring countries. The focal point of such tensions was the 2010 Association of Southeast Asian Nations (ASEAN) Regional Forum where the United States along with the ASEAN countries confronted China over its "assertive" behaviour in the South China Sea. This episode demonstrated clearly the troubled situation in the South China Sea and the potential for conflict in East Asia. [16]

Over the past two years, the United States has taken an active interest and position in what had formerly been a dispute between China and the other claimants. This means there are now in effect two layers to this dispute: a basic stand-off between the territorial claimants; and an overarching strategic contest between Beijing and Washington. For the United States, what is at stake in the South China Sea and the viability of its entire presence in the western Pacific. The U.S. Navy's access to the South China Sea is contested by Beijing. China claims it will respect the freedom of *passage* of ships and aircraft through the area, on the condition that they are en route to another destination, and do not conduct military exercises or collect intelligence or militarily useful data. Washington is adamant that the South China Sea's sea lanes are international waters, and are therefore subject to freedom of *navigation*, which in international law allows the conduct of military exercises and the collection of intelligence and militarily useful data. [17]

The United States had developed a strong alliance system with major countries of the region under the Asia-Pacific umbrella since the end of World War II. [18] The South China Sea is also bordered by a U.S. treaty ally, the Philippines, and is a key strategic waterway for the U.S. Navy. Recent examples of tensions over the SCS include a protracted standoff between China and the Philippines in the spring and summer of 2012 over a shoal known in English as Scarborough Shoal and in Chinese as Huangyan Dao. The confrontation, which began with the Philippines sending a warship to confront Chinese fishing boats near the shoal, followed a series of confrontations between the two countries in 2011.

Among the 2011 incidents was a face-off over Reed Bank, known in China as Liyue Tan, in which Chinese Maritime Surveillance ships reportedly harassed a Philippine ship conducting a seismic survey in the area. Confrontations between China and Vietnam have included two 2011 incidents in which Chinese ships cut the cables of Vietnamese oil exploration vessels. Other provocations have involved efforts to embed sovereignty claims in domestic laws and administrative structures. In June 2012, Vietnam passed a law claiming jurisdiction over two sets of island chains in the SCS, the Paracels and Spratlys, known in China as the Xisha and Nansha. On the same day, China announced the establishment of a new city on an island in the Paracels chain, Woody Island, known in China as Yongxing Dao, that it said would administer the Paracels, Spratlys, and the Macclesfield Bank, known in China as the Zhongsha. The city has its own military garrison. [19]

The U.S.-China rivalry assumed new dimensions in the context of the fact that rising China is a major claimant in the disputes. Beijing's u-shaped, nine-dashed lines lay claim to about 80 percent of the South China Sea. Washington considers Beijing's attitude and behaviour in relation to the disputes have come to be viewed as a gauge of how a strong

China may behave in the future. Such perceptions, combined with Chinese rhetoric and actions, have the potential to fuel anti-China sentiments and competitive nationalisms, reinforce historical antagonisms, and affect strategic alignments in the region. Smaller claimant countries may turn to more powerful countries like the United States to deter and counter Chinese assertiveness.

China has extensive, though imprecise, claims to large parts of the South China Sea, which is believed to be rich in oil and gas deposits as well as fisheries, and through which a major portion of world's trade passes by sea. Territory claimed by China is also claimed in part by Brunei, Malaysia, the Philippines, and Vietnam, and in entirety by Taiwan, with the fiercest territorial disputes being those between China and Vietnam and China and the Philippines. In July 2010, Secretary of State Hillary Clinton explicitly declared a U.S. "national interest" in the SCS. The State Department defines that national interest as being in "the maintenance of peace and stability, respect for international law, freedom of navigation, and unimpeded lawful commerce" in the sea. [20] The United States has said that it does not take a position on the competing sovereignty claims, but opposes "the use or threat of force by any claimant".

In her July 2010 comments at the Association of Southeast Asian Nations Regional Forum in Vietnam, Clinton said the United States was "prepared to facilitate initiatives and confidence building measures" in the area, consistent with a 2002 agreement between China and the Association of Southeast Asian Nations (ASEAN) and the ASEAN-China Declaration on the Conduct of Parties in the South China Sea. [21] The United States has since supported efforts by China's rival claimants to place the issue of the tensions in the South China Sea on the discussion agenda for regional meetings, and publicly urged ASEAN and China to move forward with long-stalled negotiations over the text of a code of conduct. On August 3, 2012, the State Department criticized China's establishment of the new city and military garrison in the South China Sea, saying the moves "run counter to collaborative diplomatic efforts to resolve differences and risk further escalating tensions in the region". [22]

The United States has also stepped up military cooperation with both the Philippines and Vietnam, in addition to announcing its policy of strategic rebalancing toward the Asia-Pacific, which includes plans to increase the proportion of U.S. warships in the Asia Pacific from 50 percent to 60 percent of the U.S. fleet, and strengthen defence ties with many of China's neighbours. China has long sought to manage its territorial disputes in the South China Sea on a bilateral basis with rival claimants, and has resisted a multilateral approach in which it might face an opposing coalition of some of these other countries. It has made clear its unhappiness with U.S. involvement in the issue, accusing the United States of complicating the situation by "internationalizing" it. Chinese commentators have also suggested that U.S. support has emboldened China's rival claimants to be more assertive in asserting their sovereignty claims. The twenty-first century will be America's Pacific century, a period of unprecedented outreach and partnership in this dynamic, complex, and consequential region. [23]

India and the South China Sea Dispute

The South China Sea dispute also dragged tension between China and India over the contested waters. As the eastern gateway to the Indian Ocean (IO), South China Sea is India's strategic left flank. And, more than half of India's interests pass through or are located in the South China Sea. India has had civilisational contacts and relations, predating the middle ages, with most of the South China Sea littoral nations. Like other major powers, India is concerned about China's challenge to the free access to the waters of the South China Sea. India has developed unprecedented strategic interest and objectives in the East Asian region especially in the areas of energy and resource security.

China considers the increased presence of India in its strategic neighbourhood as a challenge to its East Asian hegemony. China has been objecting to the Indian exploration projects in the region, claiming that the territory comes under its sovereignty. Whereas India continues to maintain that its exploration projects in the region are purely commercial, China has viewed such activities as an issue of sovereign rights. India's moves unsettled China, which views India's growing engagement in East Asia with suspicion. The South China Sea passage is too vital for trade and international security to be controlled by a single country. Meanwhile, China has been doing its best to roil the waters in the South China Sea. Concerns have been rising about China's claim to the ownership to much of the South China Sea waters and the Chinese Navy's assertive behaviour in the region.

The geostrategic significance of the South China Sea lies in the fact that it is the eastern access to the Indian Ocean. India established a presence in the South China Sea in the early days of the "Look East Policy", conducting its first-ever joint naval exercises with Indonesia (1991), Malaysia (1991), and Singapore (1993). In 2001, India held separate bilateral exercises in the South China Sea with the Vietnamese and South Korean navies. Singapore, which during the Cold War had considered the Indian navy to be a threat, reversed course in 1996 and signed an agreement on military cooperation with India. The Indian navy now conducts exercises regularly with Singapore. Thailand has developed a complementary "Look West Policy" and has become an increasingly close ally of New Delhi. Coordinated naval patrols are an element of this closer relationship. [24]

As part of its new defence strategy, India developed bilateral defence cooperation agreements with Malaysia, Singapore, Laos, and Indonesia. It has also provided military aid to the armed forces of Myanmar and Thailand. India's current maritime doctrine states that "the Indian maritime vision for the first quarter of the 21st century must look at the arc from the Persian Gulf to the Straits of Malacca as a legitimate area of interest". [25] While India's naval chief, Admiral Arun Prakash, indicated in 2005 that India had no intention of patrolling the Malacca Strait, this view changed in 2006 when New Delhi signalled its willingness to help patrol the strait subject to an invitation from the littoral states. [26]

India's rapid rise to strategic prominence in the region has been aided by its absence of any history of disputes in the region. It has no territorial claims in the region. Unlike Japan, China, or the United States, India is perceived as having no strategic ambitions in the region. It is seen as a power that could balance China's rise without posing a direct threat. However, as its trade with ASEAN and China grows, India has an increasing economic incentive to keep regional SLOCs open for international shipping. India is now embarking on Phase II of its "Look East Policy", expanding its scope to include Australia, China, Japan, and South Korea. The military contacts and joint exercises that India launched with ASEAN states on a low-key basis in the early 1990s are now expanding into full-fledged defence cooperation. [27]

Bilaterally, India regularly engages in naval exercises with the US, French, British, Russian and Singapore navies and on an opportunity basis with the Indonesian, Japanese, Philippines, Vietnamese, Saudi Arabian, German, Omani, Iranian and PLA navies. It is noteworthy that India's policy of bilateral naval engagement with a power such as the U.S. is no different at all from that with the regional or other powers. India is also distancing from the emerging rivalry of the U.S. and China over South China Sea. The challenge is for India to become a responsible balancer within the international order by effectively partnering with the key players to manage an increasingly insecure world. As a resident power in the Indian Ocean region which is still growing, India has new responsibilities in the 21st century. These relate not only to defending her own national interests but also in ensuring security and order in her maritime neighbourhood.

The Indian Maritime Military Strategy identifies the South China Sea and the Pacific Ocean as 'secondary areas' of operational interest for the Indian Navy. It elaborates, "Areas of secondary interest will come in where there is a direct connection with areas of primary interest, or where they impinge on the deployment of future maritime forces". Around 55 percent of India's trade in the Asia Pacific transits through the South China Sea region. For India, the South China Sea region serves as a strategic link between the Pacific and the Indian Oceans whose security is vital for the smooth flow of her sea borne trade. India's new energy foreign policy also gives priority for active engagement with the South China Sea littorals to commercially participate in exploration of the vital energy resources.

Any attempt by China or any other external actors to unilaterally seek to change the status quo will have the potential to impinge upon India's commercial interests relating to energy security and the navigational prerogative to freely use the South China Sea as provided for by the international law. India should also play a proactive role both strategically and diplomatically to ensure peace and order in this vital region. India's policy towards the nations involved in the South China Sea imbroglio would be to respect their viewpoints and persuade them to resolve their issues bilaterally. While not interfering in the ongoing bilateral or regional dialogues is the right policy for India, she should also hedge her bets and be ready to safeguard her own national interests. India should, therefore, extend full support to reducing friction in the region. This would be best done through principled negotiation and peaceful resolution of all potential conflicts under a defined set of rules.

Conclusions

The South China Sea is one of the most long-running and complex disputes in contemporary international affairs. It remains one of the few flashpoints around the globe that holds the potential to directly escalate into a great power conflict. China is on a trajectory to become the emerging maritime power in the twenty first century. China has the potential to reshape the global balance power and the U.S. dominance in the evolving global strategic landscape. The South China Sea dispute emerged as a new area of conflict between the rising China and other major powers of the world. Sea lines of communication of the South China Sea are vital for the economic development of Asia-Pacific countries. The South China Sea's vast energy resources in the heavily disputed Spratly and Paracel Island regions stand to raise the stakes of interested parties including the U.S. and India. Given China's rise and its territorial claims to not only the Islands, but the vast majority of the South China Sea and its resources, it remains unclear whether such claims will become a platform for cooperation or conflict.

The South China Sea symbolises rising China's larger strategic dilemma in the emerging global security order. For China, the South China Sea dispute represents the kind of challenge that could determine whether or how China will indeed ascend to superpower status. Regrettably, China does not yet recognize the extent to which its aggressive course in the South China Sea is damaging its diplomacy with neighbouring countries. China had showed its assertiveness in the South China Sea through a tough posture instead of a conciliatory approach of diplomacy and economic integration with its Southeast Asian neighbours. Other South China Sea states are also asserting their own claims and developing their own naval capacity, albeit to a lesser degree than China. As the eastern gateway to the Indian Ocean, South China Sea is India's strategic left flank. And, more than half of India's interests pass through or are located in the South China Sea. Any attempt to destabilize the region will have serious national security challenges for India.

India should strongly push for the freedom of navigation in

the maritime commons. It is of paramount importance that status quo be maintained in respect of freedom of access and passage within the South China Sea., Managing the South China Sea dispute requires both a deeper understanding of the sources and drivers of conflicts, and the development of mechanisms, in bilateral and multilateral settings, to address them. How China, India and the United States respond to the rising tensions and strategic miscalculations in their South China Sea policy will significantly influence international relations in the coming decades. China's handling of sovereignty disputes with some of its neighbours, and differences with the U.S. and India has already weakened its standing in East Asia and beyond. Given the critical importance of the South China Sea in the national security calculus of the various stakeholders and the absence of a viable mechanism to understand and address these emerging security challenges will certainly influence the emerging strategic and security order in the new century.

Endnotes

1. The South China Sea is a recurrent flashpoint in the Asia Pacific region that has recently threatened to destabilize the East Asian regional security order. The 21st ASEAN Summit, 2012 once again brought South China Sea dispute to the fore of internal bickering among the ASEAN member countries and also reflects the growing divide among the major global powers over the disputed strategic waters. The Chairman's statement of the 21st ASEAN Summit meeting underlined the importance of Declaration on the Conduct of Parties in South China Sea Dispute and (2002) and ASEAN's Six-Point Principles on South China Sea dispute (2012). It also called upon the member states for peaceful resolution of the dispute 'through consultations and negotiations by sovereign states directly concerned'. While Cambodia declared that ASEAN had agreed not to 'internationalise the South China Sea issue', reflecting China's position, the Philippino delegation expressed reservations over such an agreement among the ASEAN member states and asserted its sovereign right to defend its territorial interests in a

manner as it saw fit. The Philippines called upon the U.S. to play a greater role in the resolution of the dispute. The 21st ASEAN Summit also provided greater regional and international legitimacy to both the ASEAN framework and its demand for a binding Code of Conduct over the South China Sea dispute. For more details, see Vibhanshu Shekhar (2012), 21st ASEAN Summit 2012: Key Outcomes, www.icwa.in.

2. For more details, see Michael Leifer, "The Maritime Regime and Regional Security in East Asia", *Pacific Review* 4 (1991): 126-136. See also, more recently, Sam Bateman, "Building Good Order at Sea in Southeast Asia: The Promise of International Regimes" in 'Maritime Security in Southeast Asia', (eds.) Kwa Chong Guan and John K. Skogan, London: Routledge, 2007, 97-116.
3. The 1982 Convention on the Law of Seas has numerous guidelines pertaining to islands, the continental shelf, enclosed seas and territorial limits. Pertinent articles as applicable to this dispute are Articles 3, 55-75, 76 and 121. Article 3 establishes that every state has the right to establish the breadth of its territorial sea up to a limit not exceeding 12 nautical miles. Articles 55-75 explain the concept of Exclusive Economic Zone (EEZ), which is an area up to 200 nautical miles beyond and adjacent to the territorial sea. The EEZ gives coastal states sovereign rights for the purpose of exploring, exploiting, conserving and managing the natural resources. Article 76 defines the continental shelf of a nation which comprises the sea and subsoil of the submarine areas that extend beyond its territorial sea throughout the natural prolongation of its land territory to the outer edge of the continental margin, or to a distance of 200 nautical missiles. This is significant as it allows every nation to exploit the continental shelf. Article 121 states that rocks that cannot sustain human habitation or economic life shall have no EEZ or continental shelf. In the case of the South China Sea, most of the claimants have established military outposts in order to conform to Article 121 in pressing their claims. The Convention also states that overlapping claims must be resolved in good faith. For more details See United Nations Convention on the Law of the Sea, 1833 *U.N.T.S.* 397, Article 122; Sam Bateman, Ralf Emmers (2012), "Security and International Politics in the South China Sea: Towards a co-

operative Management Regime", Routledge; Harsh V. Pant (2012), South China Sea: New Arena of Sino-Indian Rivalry, Yale Global, August 2.

4. Eric Talmadge, "Battle for Control of Asia's Seas Goes Underwater", *The Straits Times*, January 19, 2012, available at: http://www.straitstimes.com/BreakingNews/Asia/Story/STIStory_757506.html.
5. John H. Noer and David Gregory, "Chokepoints: Maritime Economic Concerns in Southeast Asia", Washington DC: NDU Press, 1996, Figures 17-20, 63-66.
6. United Nations Environment Programme (UNEP), "Global International Waters Assessment", South China Sea: Regional Assessment 54, Kalmar, Sweden: University of Kalmar, 2005, 40-41.
7. This term was coined by a U.S. report, "Energy Futures in Asia", produced by consultants Booz Allen Hamilton for the Office of the Secretary of Defence. A string of ports, bases, and listening posts stretching from the entrance to the Persian Gulf through to the South China Sea constitute the so-called "pearls". The report was first publicised by Bill Gertz, "China Builds up Strategic Sea Lanes", *Washington Times*, January 18, 2005.
8. Some of these are historically based, such as between Singapore and Malaysia; related to territorial or maritime disputes, such as that between Indonesia and Malaysia over the Ambalat offshore development area on the east coast of Borneo; or both, such as the nascent Philippine claim to Sabah or the long-standing enmity and distrust between Vietnam and China. Religious and ethnic factors may also play a role in some rivalries. Even though many of the rival states would never admit to it, such relationships are factors in military modernization.
9. For more details, see Toshi Yoshihara and James R. Holmes, "Red Star over the Pacific: China's Rise and the Challenge to U.S. Maritime Strategy", Annapolis, Naval Institute Press, 2010, 51-53.
10. An energy importer since 1993, China's high energy demand has prompted it to intensify offshore exploration, including a tripartite seismic survey in the South China Sea with the Philippines and Vietnam; to acquire or invest in exploration and production projects overseas; to enter into supply contracts with countries as diverse as Angola, Australia, Iran, Sudan, and

Venezuela; and to establish a strategic oil reserve.

11. China's historical claims to the South China Sea date back to the Han and Ming Dynasties. For a detailed discussion on the Spratly Island dispute and territorial claims, see Michael W. King, "United States and the Spratly Islands: Six Actors, Which Stage?", Strategy Research Project, Carlisle Barracks, PA: U.S. Army War College, November 24, 2001, 1-21; Also see, Country Analysis Briefs for the South China Sea, available at: http://search.usa.gov/search?affiliate=eia.doe.gov&v%3Aproject=firstgov&query=spratly+islands.
12. For a detailed listing, see "Country Analysis Briefs for the South China Sea", available at: http://search.usa.gov/search?affiliate=eia.doe.gov&v%3Aproject=firstgov&query=spratly+islands.
13. Under the UNCLOS, states have sovereign rights to explore, exploit, conserve, and manage the natural resources within an EEZ which can range to 200 nautical miles (nms) beyond a state's territorial sea. China's loose interpretation of the UNCLOS has permitted it to claim territory and establish an EEZ that stretches to nearly 1,000 nms beyond mainland China and encroaches upon the sovereignty of its neighbours. Notably, most of the Spratly Islands are submerged at high tide and do no meet the legal criteria necessary for EEZs. Furthermore, although a signatory to the UNCLOS, China unilaterally established its own measure through its 1992 Law on Territorial Waters and their Contiguous Areas. This solidified the Chinese claim to the Spratly and Parcel islands as well as empowered the People's Liberation Army (PLA) to employ force to defend the islands. Citing this, UNCLOS, and historical records, China claims ownership of roughly 80 percent of the South China Sea including areas that encompass existing oil fields operated by Brunei and Indonesia. China bases such claims on historical references to exploration, naming, utilization, government jurisdiction, and acceptance of the Japanese surrender following World War II to validate its sovereign control of the area, yet this isn't codified anywhere in international law. See, Article 57 of UNCLOS prescribes a 200nm limit to any Exclusive Economic Zone (EEZ), available at: http://www.un.org/Depts/los/convention_agreements/convention overview_convention.htm;

"Why ASEAN Should Align Themselves Against China", January 31, 2008, available at:
http://www.paracelspratly.com;
Michael T. Klare (2001), "Resource Wars: The New Landscape of Global Conflict", New York, NY: Henry Hold and Company, LLC., 121; Xavier Furtado, "International Law and the Dispute over the Spratly Islands: Whither UNCLOS?", *Contemporary Southeast Asia*, December 1999, 386-404.

14. Daniel T. Kate, and Nicole Gaouette, "Clinton Signals U.S. Role in China Territorial Disputes after ASEAN", July 23, 2010, available at:
http://www.bloomberg.com/news/2010-07-23/u-s-says-settling-south-china-sea-disputes-leading-diplomatic-priority-.html.
15. The United States has had an extensive history with Asian nations over the past century, and every action in the South China Sea is viewed through this historic lens. The opening of Japan (1853), the Boxer Rebellion (1899-1901), the Philippine-American War (1899-1902), the Asiatic Fleet (1902-1942), The Flying Tigers (1941-1942), World War II (1939-1945), Sino-American Mutual Defence Treaty (1955), the Korean War (1950-1953), and the Vietnam War (1950-1975) are just a few historical events that shape U.S.'s role in and perception of Asia's geopolitics.
16. Robert D. Kaplan, writing on how the issue will be a major challenge for the future, states, "Just as German soil constituted the military front line of the Cold War, the waters of the South China Sea may constitute the military front line of the coming decades". Kaplan, Robert D., "The South China Sea is the Future of Conflict", Foreign Policy, September/October 2011.
17. Peter Dutton, "Three Disputes and Three Objectives: China and the South China Sea", *Naval War College Review*, 64(4), Autumn 2011, 54-55. If Washington surrenders its ability to navigate the South China Sea on its own terms, it will lose a major foothold in the western Pacific.
18. The United States has signed defence treaties with Australia, Japan, South Korea, Thailand, New Zealand, and the Philippines. U.S. military relationships have been strengthened with many ASEAN members including Brunei, Cambodia, Indonesia, Laos, Malaysia, Vietnam, and Singapore. Recent negotiations have enabled the United States to base warships in

Singapore and the same is expected to occur in the Philippines. With regard to China, diplomatic relations have significantly improved over the last twenty years, but various military incidents indicate shortcomings in Sino-U.S. relations. The U.S. EP-3 reconnaissance aircraft's collision with a Chinese Shenyang J-8 fighter aircraft followed by a crash landing on Hainan Island in April 2001, cancellation of a planned port visit in Hong Kong by the aircraft carrier USS Kitty Hawk and two minesweepers by the PRC Ministry of Foreign Affairs in November 2007, the harassment of U.S Navy ocean surveillance ships USNS Victorious and USNS Impeccable by multiple Chinese vessels and aircraft in March 2009, and the "inadvertent encounter" (collision) of a Chinese submarine with the towed sonar array of the USS John McCain off the Philippine coast in June 2009 are a few examples of incidents that have sparked U.S. concern in the South China Sea. See Barbara Star, "Sub Collides with Sonar Array Towed by U.S. Navy Ship", *CNN*, June 12, 2009, available at: http://articles.cnn.com/2009-06-12/us/china.submarine_1_navy-ship-sonar-array-chinese-vessels?_s=PM:US.

19. International Crisis Group, "Stirring Up the South China Sea (II): Regional Responses", Asia Report No. 229, July 24, 2012, available at: http://www.crisisgroup.org/en/regions/asia/north-east-asia/china/229-stirring-up-the-south-china-sea-iiregional-responses.aspx.
20. U.S. Department of State, Patrick Ventrell, Acting Deputy Spokesperson, Office of Press Relations: Statement on the South China Sea, August 3, 2012, available at: http://www.state.gov/r/pa/prs/ps/2012/08/196022.htm.
21. Remarks at Press Availability, Hillary Rodham Clinton, Secretary of State, National Convention Centre, Hanoi, Vietnam, July 23, 2010, available at: http://www.state.gov/secretary/rm/2010/07/145095.htm.

The text of the Declaration on the Conduct of Parties In the South China Sea, available at: http://www.aseansec.org/13163.htm.

ASEAN comprises 10 Southeast Asian nations: Brunei, Cambodia, Indonesia, Lao, Malaysia, Myanmar, Philippines, Singapore, Thailand, Vietnam.

22. U.S. Department of State, "Patrick Ventrell, Acting Deputy Spokesperson, Office of Press Relations: Statement on the South China Sea," August 3, 2012, available at: http://www.state.gov/r/pa/prs/ps/2012/08/196022.htm.
23. For a detailed account of the changing dimensions of U.S.-Asia Pacific policy, see Hillary Rodham Clinton, "America's Pacific Century", East-West Centre, Honolulu, HI, November 10, 2011.
24. For details, see Faizal Yahya (2003), "India and Southeast Asia Revisited", *Contemporary Southeast Asia*, 25:7.
25. Integrated Headquarters, Ministry of Defence (Navy), "Indian Maritime Doctrine", INBR 8, New Delhi: Integrated Headquarters, Ministry of Defence, 2004, 56.
26. "India Has No Intention of Patrolling Malacca Straits", *Daily Times,* July 23, 2005.
27. India-ASEAN Summit, India-ASEAN Summit Declaration, 30 November 2004, New Delhi.

References

Amit Singh (2011), "South China Sea Disputes: Regional Issues, Global Concerns, Maritime Affairs", *Journal of the National Maritime Foundation of India*, Vol. 1, Issue 1.

Amitav Acharya (2013), "ASEAN 2030: Challenges of Building a Mature Political and Security Community", ADBI Working Paper, Asian Development Bank Institute, Tokyo, No. 441, available at: http://www.adbi.org/files/2013.10.25.wp441.asean.2030.political.security.community.pdf.

A. Bergsten, (2006), "China the Balance Sheet: What the World Needs to Know now about the Emerging Superpower", New York: Public Affairs.

Clive Schofield (2009), "Dangerous Ground: A Geopolitical Overview of the South China Sea", in 'Security and International Politics in the South China Sea: Towards a Cooperative Management Regime', (eds.) Sam Bateman and Ralf Emmers, London: Routledge, 14-18.

David Rosenberg (2010), "Governing the South China Sea: From Freedom of the Seas to Ocean Enclosure Movements", *Harvard Asia Quarterly*, December 26, available at: http://asiaquarterly.com/2010/12/26/governing-the-south-china-sea-from-freedom-of-the-seas-to-ocean-enclosure-movements/

David Rosenberg and Christopher Chung (2008), "Maritime Security in the South China Sea: Coordinating Coastal and User State Priorities", *Ocean Development and International Law*, 39:51-68.

David Zweig and Jianhai Bi (2005), "China's Global Hunt for Energy", *Foreign Affairs,* 84(5): 25-38.

Denny Roy (2012), "South China Sea: Not Just About Free Navigation", *Asia Pacific Bulletin*, No. 17, August 14.

Dingli Shen (2013), "Reconciliation in the South China Sea", in Ron Huisken (ed.), 'CSCAP Regional Security Outlook 2014', The Council for Security Cooperation in the Asia Pacific (CSCAP), Kuala Lumpur, available at: http://www.cscap.org/uploads/docs/CRSO/CRSO2014.pdf.

Gunther Hauser and Franz Kernic (eds.) (2009), "China: The Rising Power", Frankfurt am Main, Berlin, Bern, Bruxelles, New York, Oxford, Wien.

Harsh Pant (2009), "Indian Foreign Policy in a Unipolar World", London: Routledge.

J. Nye (2005), "Understanding International Conflicts: An Introduction to Theory and History", New York: Pearson/Longman.

John Ikenberry (2008), "The Rise of China and the Future of the West: Can the Liberal System Survive?", *Foreign Affairs,* 87, No. 1, January/February.

John C. Daly (2012), "China's Benign Foreign Policy Image at Odds with South China Sea Stance", *Refinery News*, February 20, available at: http://refinerynews.com/chinas-benign-foreign-policy-image-at-odds-with-south-china-sea-stance.

L.C. Russell Hsiao (2009), "In a Fortnight: PLA General Advises Building Bases in the South China Sea", Jamestown Foundation, *China Brief,* 24 June, 1-2.

L.H. Hamilton (2005), foreword in J.H. Kalicki and D.L. Goldwyn (eds.), 'Energy and Security: Toward a New Foreign Policy Strategy', Washington: Woodrow Wilson Centre Press, xxi.

L. Hancher, and S. Janssen (2004), "Shared Competences and Multi-Faceted Concepts: European Legal Framework for Security of Supply", in B. Barton, C. Redgwell, A. Ronne, and D.N. Zillman (eds.), 'Energy Security: Managing Risk in a Dynamic Legal and Regulatory Environment', Oxford: Oxford University

Press, 85-119.

Leszek Buszyinski (2012), "The South China Sea: Oil, Maritime Claims, and U.S.-China Strategic Rivalry", *The Washington Quarterly*, 35:2, 139-156, Spring.

Marquis Clayton (2012), "Uncomfortable Truths: Breaking the Impasse in the South China Sea", *Asia Pacific Bulletin*, Number 178, August 24.

M.T. Klare (2008), "Rising Powers, Shrinking Planet: The New Geopolitics of Energy", New York: Metropolitan Books.

Peter Dutton (2011), "Three Disputes and Three Objectives: China and the South China Sea", *Naval War College Review,* 64, No. 4, 42-67.

Ralf Emmers (2010), "Geopolitics and Maritime Territorial Disputes in East Asia", London; New York: Routledge.

Sam Bateman and Ralf Emmers (2012), "Security and International Politics in the South China Sea: Towards a Co-operative Management Regime", Routledge.

Steve Hargreaves (2012), "Tensions Heat Up Over Oil, Gas in South China Sea", *CNN*, April 26, available at: http://money.cnn.com/2012/04/24/news/economy/south-china-sea/index.htm.

Yunchang Jeffrey Bor and Zhong Xiang Zhang (2010), "Energy Economics: Asian Energy in the Context of Growing Security and Environmental Concerns".

Index

Index

A

Ajit Doval, 44
Al Ummah, 81
Arabian Sea, 21, 42
Arthasastra, 39
Arun Prakash, 19, 20
ASEAN (Association of Southeast Asian Nations), 8
Association for Defence Companies (ADC), 56
Atal Behari Vajpayee, 7, 24

B

Bay of Bengal, 21, 42
Bharat Karnad, 33
BIMSTEC (Bangladesh, India, Myanmar, Sri Lanka and Thailand Economic Cooperation), 8
Binori Madrasa, 81
Blue Economy, 27
Brahma Chellany, 16
Brahmnical Hinduism, 43
BRICS (Brazil, Russia, India, China and South Africa), 37
Bretton Woods institutions, 35

C

C. Raja Mohan, 16
Cape of Good Hope, 21
China National Electronic Import and Export Corporation (CNEIEC), 80
Chinese Aerospace Long–March International Trade (CALMIT), 80
Cinderella Service, 53
Coastal Security Scheme, 92
Cold War, 1, 9, 76, 86, 169
Colombo Port Expansion Project, 129
Condolesa Rice, 41
Contingency Reserve Arrangement (CRA), 38
Cultural Revolution (1966-76), 150

D

D.K. Joshi, 54
Declaration on Strategic Partnership 2000, 106
Devin Hagerty, 32
Dharmasala Conference of Chinese Dissidents, 33
Dhruv Light Combat Helicopter, 109
Diego Garcia, 77
Director General Coast Guard, 61
Donald Henry Rumsfeld, 126

Dubai Port World (DPW), 25

E

Embedded Liberalism, 37
Emerging World Order, 2
Energy Security, 26
Euro-Atlantic world, 19
European Union, 2
Exclusive Economic Zone (EEZ), 90

F

Fuel Folio, 58

G

General Agreement on Trade and Services (GATS), 45
Goldman Sachs, 33
Gujral Doctrine, 41, 45
Gulf of Hormuz, 21

H

Harsh V. Pant, 32
Hindu Cultural Nationalism, 43
Hydrocarbon Vision 2020, 26

I

India-China Border Dispute, 154
Indian Border Security Forces, 120
Indian Diaspora, 6
Indian Maritime Doctrine 2009, 18, 27
Indian Maritime Military Strategy, 177
Indian National Congress, 32, 40
Indian Ocean Region (IOR), 22
Indian Ocean, 20, 41
Indira Doctrine, 45
Indira Gandhi, 36, 40
Indo-Soviet Treaty of Friendship 1971, 106
INS Kadmatt, 56
INS Kalvari, 56
INS Kamorta, 56
INS Sindhurakshak, 53
INS Vikramaditya, 18, 53
INS Viraat, 53
Institute for Defence Studies and Analyses, 109
Intercontinental Ballistic Missiles (ICBMs), 12
International Container Transhipment Terminal (ICTT), 25
International Covenant on Economic Social and Cultural Rights, 145
International Covenants on Civil and Political Rights, 145
International Maritime Boundary Line (IMBL), 61

International Maritime Organisation (IMO), 62
International Ship and Port Facility Security (ISPS), 93
Port Management and Ocean Management, 62
International Ship and Port Facility Security Code, 63
IORA (Indian Ocean Rim Association), 29
Italian Marine, 86

J

Jawaharlal Nehru, 152

K

K. Subrahmaniam, 83
K.M. Panikkar, 20, 72, 124
K.R. Singh, 95

L

Liberalisation, Privatisation and Globalisation (LPG), 42
Liberation Tigers of Tamil Eelam, 120
Logistics Exchange Memorandum of Agreement (LEMOA), 44
Logistics Support Agreement (LSA), 44
Lok Sabha, 29
Long Range Identification System (LRIT), 94
Look East Policy, 8, 42, 175

M

M.S. Golvalker, 43
Mahavir Singh, 16
Make-in-India, 55, 56
Malacca Strait, 176
Manmohan Singh, 7, 25, 33, 37, 42
Maritime Century, 30
Maritime Domain Awareness (MDA), 18
Maritime Military Strategy (2007), 21
Maritime Security, 19
Maritime Silk Road, 78
Maritime Silk Route (MSR), 30, 78
Marshal Plan, 78
Maulana Abul Kalam Azad Institute of Asian Studies, 16
Mazagon Docks, 56
McMohan Line, 151
Mekong-Ganga Initiative, 8
Mig 21, 104
Ministry of Defence, 27
Ministry of External Affairs (MEA), 29
Ministry of Home Affairs, 92
Ministry of New and

Renewable Energy, 29
Modernization of Armed Forces, 12
Modi Doctrine, 43, 45
Monroe Doctrine, 36
Multi-Barrel Rocket Launcher Smerch, 107

N
Nalini Kant Jha, 16
Narasimha Rao, 33, 34, 37, 40, 49
Narendra Modi, 34, 43, 49, 130
National Institutes for Oceanography, 62
National Maritime Authority, 29
National Oil Spill Disaster Contingency Plans (NOSDCP), 61
National Security Advisory Board (NSAB), 10
National Solar Mission, 26
New Development Bank (NDB), 38
New International Economic Order (NIEO), 36
Nirmal Sitaraman, 45
Non-Aligned Movement (NAM), 9
Novosti Press, 77
Nuclear Suppliers Group (NSG), 1

O
Obama Administration, 3
Ocean Technology, 62
One Belt, One Road (OBOR), 78

P
Pakistani High Commission, 81
Palk Bay, 61
People's Liberation Army (PLA), 150, 167
Persian Gulf, 9, 21
Pinak Ranjan Chakravarty, 123
Piracy in Somalia, 76
Pokharan, 11
Post-Cold War World, 1
Pradeep Chauhan, 31
Prakash Karat, 34

R
R.K. Dhowan, 56
Rajan Mathai, 105
Rani Durgavati, 54
Ranil Wickremesinghe, 73
Red Sea, 21
Red Sea-Suez Canal Passage, 19
Reed Bank, 172
Rio Declaration, 28

S
Sagarmala, 24
Sarva Daman Singh, 16
Sea-lanes of

Communications (SLOC), 27
Second World War, 76
Sethu Samudram Ship Canal Project, 63
Sethusamudram Canal Project, 25
Shimla Convention of 1914, 152
Shyam Saran, 38
South China Sea, 21, 162
Southern Indian Ocean, 21
South-South cooperation, 42
Stephen Cohen, 5
Strait of Babel-el-Mandeb, 21
Strait of Malacca, 21
Sulzan Energy, 29
Sunil Khilnani, 16
Suresh Mehta, 27

T

Tablighi Jamaat, 81
Taliban in Afghanistan, 3
Third World, 9
Tibetan Refugees in India, 153
Tropic of Cancer, 75

U

U.N. Security Council, 10
UN General Assembly, 9, 142
United Nations Conference on Sustainable Development, 28
United Nations World Conference on Human Rights, 146
United Nations, 10
United Progressive Alliance (UPA), 37
Universal Declaration of Human Rights (UDHR), 144

V

Vasco de Gama, 20
Vasudhaiva Kutumbakam, 5

W

Wall Street-WTO-World Bank Complex, 47
Walter Lipmann, 16
World Bank, 35
World Trade Organization (WTO), 14

Y

Yang Jiechi, 44
Yield-to-weight (Y/W) Ratio, 12

Z

Zardari Government of Pakistan, 11
Zhao Nanqi, 74